Ken Burgess

Entrepreneurs Won't Cry

GW00391361

Says Ken Burgess

Entrepreneurs Won't Cry

Ken Burgess

Dedication

I dedicate my book to "My Old Granny" (MOGUS), who played an important role in my early education.

What would she have said after reading the book?

Probably this: "Your goal is not always going to be within your reach as at times you have to outstretch yourself to reach it. Furthermore, equality is not regarding different things similarly; equality is regarding different things DIFFERENTLY.

People generally define success in different ways that is why it is very important that all parties wishing to succeed in their lives and opportunities accurately define what their venture is about and is made understandable to those parties you wish to get support from. However, it is important that you accept constructive criticism and its benefits, such as opportunities and ambition."

Alternatively, she may have said, "Money does not grow on trees, you know!"

Acknowledgements

I want to thank the people and companies who have invested in products and ideas that I have been involved with and appreciate them as they lent their enthusiasm and encouragement when I needed it!

To my previous partners, especially the late Roy Simpson and Gerry Cullimore with Paul Carter and John Oxley, all mentioned in the book (not the ones I have unfulfilled business with!)

To Athena Wan, my long-suffering accountant and business partner in VIIL, not forgetting my old friend, Michael Linnit, whose ideas in our youth to make money will never be forgotten.

To the Three Ladies who have played an important part in my business life: Gloria Simpson as a business partner and loyal PA, Elisabeth Cooper, for she steadfastly supported me throughout the good and troubling times.

To my ex-wife, Tina Burgess, who has been outstanding as a Mother to our Sons and pacifier to me during the early stages of my business career.

To my Sons, Simon and Daniel, for their constructive 'Criticism and Input,' coupled with their determination to succeed in their business developments, and for that, I am very proud of their success and support that they continually give to third parties.

Ken Burgess

To Peter Knight Jnr, who was the best man at my wedding and always had time to spur me on when I was down.

To The Times Newspaper, especially Raconteur, as I used some of their data produced on technology.

And last but not least, to the late Chairman of the Shanning Group, Ron Botting, for his tenacity, diligence, and guidance.

Table of Contents

Dedication iii

Acknowledgements iv

Introductions: Entrepreneurs Won't Cry & MOGUS 1

True Entrepreneurs 8

My Early Introduction To Business..13

Onwards, upwards & even downwards! 19

Consider A Business Partnership?..48

    What makes a good partnership?..48

    New and improved technology introduces new opportunities..............52

Am I Entrepreneurial? 57

Start as you mean to go on..71

Feasibility Study/Research 78

The Business Plan 85

Product Name or Brand? 93

"Clear Change" - Goals..96

Enterprising Oldies...98

    Key points to remember when starting a business 101

Business fraud or fraud for life?...104

New Business Opportunities?...110

Improvisation..113

In Conclusion 115

Introductions: Entrepreneurs Won't Cry & MOGUS

The word entrepreneur comes from the **French word entreprendre-** "to undertake." The Oxford dictionary defines it as a contractor acting as an intermediary between labour and capital! I completely endorse the definitions because it is my experience that they are totally different people with different ambitions, personalities, and objectives. The first use of the word entrepreneur is credited to an Irish economist called Richard Cantillon, who, in 1730, believed that the word defined equal balance between any powers, influences, etc.

Today, many definitions and ideas are linked to innovation, from taking risks to producing and executing ideas that one's maximize success in their business endeavour.

The book is a serious but hopefully humorous attempt to define and assist those who believe they have what it takes to become a successful entrepreneur, or have they?

As many academics will tell you, many successful businesspersons (not entrepreneurs) define the true entrepreneurial business person. However, the vast majority have never been involved in a new business venture where they have had to put their own money on the line in the pursuit and courage of their conviction. It is my opinion that they are confused with the reality of starting one's own company, as opposed to the entrepreneurial person who has an insatiable desire to make money; by developing or converting their ideas into product or products, which generally lead to the inevitable creation and development of a company or companies, both successful and unfortunately - unsuccessful!

Would-be entrepreneurs come in all shapes and sizes, or should I say age and gender. Age is not necessarily a deterrent but more of what I would call a reduction in risk power! Neither is the lack of formal education; it can be the incentive to succeed in some cases.

A result of the Corona Virus Pandemic and all that the world is having to endure has, without doubt, changed the way that businesses, both new and established, will and are already being run. New products, start-up opportunities are already being researched in many different parts of the world, potentially making 2022 a very active period for early-stage start-ups. And that implies, now more than ever, the importance of setting up the company the right way.

Although developing technology is substantially influenced by the advent of Social Media (and all that it entails), we increasingly see that basic corporate requirements have not. They have become even more important in attracting investment and running the business efficiently from initial seed/ feasibility and hopefully on to – an early-stage start-up.

Have you got what it takes?

Viability of the "it can't fail" idea: Setting out the stall for would-be investors: The importance of the name game:

Partnerships the pros and cons: Marketing creates and Sales satisfies: Start as you mean to go on: Cash flow is king:

'A HARD DAYS YEAR': *Dedication is not enough:*

When all else fails: Dilution is a dirty word: Sell the wife (or husband) but keep the car: Staying power: review a winning team: Don't fall in love with the company!

The book reflects on two key aspects. The main aspect is that Entrepreneurs won't cry. This aspect reflects my positive and negative experiences over 60 years of researching, forming, developing, establishing, and running those companies, which entailed successes and failures! I describe the real highs and the lows, the fun, and the tears, the gains and the losses of developing an actual idea from seed to start-up, which then hopefully progresses through to early-stage and eventually into successful maturity if the idea passes seed/feasibility. Then the book moves on to the mechanics of start-up, the expansion, funding, and ongoing development of the company.

My Old Granny Used to Say (MOGUS)

Virtually, every aspect of my business career has been influenced by **"My Old Granny Used to Say"** (MOGUS), covering many aspects of business life, the lessons learned, and benefits gained when using sayings that were directly linked to the experience or situation as defined Entrepreneurs Won't Cry (EWC); literally, two books in one? Let's say, "One and a half," as MOGUS would say.

> "Tell me & I forget, Show me & I remember, involve me, and I learn." (Benjamin Franklin)

Almost everybody has or had a Granny (or Grand-Dad) who, in varying degrees, good or bad, was an influence in, or to, their lives. It may have been discipline, humour, even antagonism. They may have been your greatest fan or negatively influenced your life.

MOGUS – became a virtual symbol of greeting or humour to clients worldwide. Many a negotiation would either start or end with MOGUS. It broke the ice during stalemate situations, and many a deal, regardless of that person's nationality, colour, or creed would end with a statement & MOGUS. As years progressed, clients globally would try to get in first with MOGUS. What did she say? Everything! "My Old Granny" had a saying for virtually every situation.

As a child, I did not understand the majority of the meanings or the value of the message that they portrayed, let alone how valuable they would become in reminding me of life's uncertainties and opportunities and, above all, that there are two sides (in some countries that I shall not name there are three sides) to every situation... or story!

As time went on, I did realize that the majority of my Old Granny's saying were quotes made by other people, which and where possible, I acknowledge accordingly. I would also say that when experiencing a low, depressive, tiered, frustrating period, thinking of a particular MOGUS bought a smile to my face! My old Granny's sayings found great parity with clients throughout the world, which becomes apparent during the book & in hindsight, maybe I should have branded "My old Granny used to say" as it reflects the importance or influence which those sayings held and their part in business education which are reflected throughout the book.

MOGUS: Don't let your struggle be your identity – *"It is not the strongest of the species who survive nor the most intelligent but the one most responsive to change." (Darwin)*

This book reflects, in two parts, the very personal and honest reflection of the business life, Ken Burgess, and my honest views relating to my experience in researching, developing, establishing, and or investing in new business ideas and opportunities over a 50 plus year period.

It covers my family (MOGUS) influence, my first investment at age 13, the escapades, both highs, and lows, of early jobs through to the development of some 50+, new company start-ups/early-stage over 60+ years. It details a wide and varied range of experiences from early days of developing new technology for Central Pipe Medical Gas and Alarm systems for hospitals and automated pneumatic systems with our start-up company Applied Pneumatic systems (APS). Moving on to negotiating new business opportunities for our "Total Turnkey" – Hospital projects, Nursing Homes, Eye Academies & Sports fitness and injury centres in the UK, Middle East, Africa, and Asia, whilst dealing with Multinational Corporations, the DTI, Governments, their ministers and Export Credit departments to name but a few.

I also reflect on my early exposure to the Internet (with my Sons) via Space FM Internet radio, targeting the Youth Market, to the current interest in the development of Social Media across a section of the companies and products developed, plus new ideas and developments into technology-related start-ups from Internet Radio, TV, OTT, Software Communications, let alone Livetime2 Limited, arguably the potential of being a global giant that after some eight years of, on/off, development abruptly ended due to several individuals' incompetence & illegal actions.

Finally, I expand on what I believe are the salient points and actions required when reviewing priorities as to whether one's idea is viable or otherwise and, if seemingly positive, the actions required to take that Idea to the next phase of starting that company, its brand, funding and ongoing development.

Last but not least, I advise on the inherent pitfalls along the way that a developing Entrepreneur will face and give recommendations when addressing them.

True Entrepreneurs

Entrepreneurs are like professional salespersons, actors, and sportspersons. They are born with an innate drive, passion, and will to succeed. Given the right opportunities and support, they can, and many do, fine-tune those basic instincts, with some, to the point of perfection.

However, suppose those traits are not there naturally, even when the best intentions are coupled with limitless investment. In that case, one may produce a businessperson, but it is my opinion that what you will not produce is a successful Entrepreneur.

How do I know?

I have met many successful business persons who have established a very successful business and whose life revolves around that business. I would not consider it Entrepreneurial.

It is, however, my opinion that the overwhelming majority are not Entrepreneurs. An Entrepreneur likes the challenge of developing an idea into a business but generally speaking could, at a certain time, be encouraged to bring in a new party or parties to run that business enabling "him or her" to spend more time on developing "that new idea" and so on.

In my experience, Entrepreneurs, even if they are the Founders of that business, do not necessarily make the best 'hands-on'

Chairperson or even CEO' in the long term. They generally take up the role of 'Executive Chairperson' as per the likes of **Elon Musk,** who, as Chairman and CEO of Tesla, recently handed over his Chairmanship of Tesla while driving the company as its Chief Executive.

Musk has many involvements, including SpaceX. As of January 2021, Tesla's market capitalization was more than $800 billion. Musk's history is truly Entrepreneurial; born in South Africa, arrived in Canada at age 17, and then on to university in the US. In 1995, Elon & his brother Kimble started ZIP2, a dot com publishing business. In 1999, they sold that company for $300 million. He then set up a company X.com, which turned into PayPal, to which he sold his shareholding to eBay for $200 million. Currently, Musk is recognised as one of the world's richest men with a personal fortune in excess of $188 billion!

Musk could have retired, but being a true Entrepreneur, he has a relentless work ethic and started on several new concepts from Space exploration with SpaceX in 2002 and in February 2004, invested in Electric cars – Tesla which in 2003 was initially founded by two US engineers, Eberhard and Terpening. The rest is history with Musk investing substantially in taking a controlling interest and in shaping, developing, and driving the company.

In 2008, Musk nearly lost all his money on launching new business projects; he had borrowed a lot of money from friends and was also forced to sleep in friends' spare rooms. He states that the Sunday before Xmas of that year, he was at his lowest ebb and true to his Entrepreneurial spirit says that the next morning, NASA called, stating that they wanted SpaceX to resupply their Space station. He was on a high. I feel sure that all his emotions were also on a high when on May 30th, 2020, he watched the thunder of rocket engines and the sight of SpaceX rocket blasting into the sky carrying two American astronauts to the International Space Station, followed by the first commercial flight for NASA with the successful launch of 4 Astronauts to the space station on November 15th, 2020.

In addition, his company, Starlink Satellites, sent 12,000 satellites into low earth orbit to deliver superfast broadband to internet black spots. Starlink is already providing a million dishes across rural areas in the US and could shortly be targeting the UK.

Musk, without a doubt, epitomises the name Entrepreneur and is a genius in his field with an insatiable appetite for developing ideas/companies. He recently announced on Twitter an incentive (prize) of $100 million for the best technology to capture and store carbon dioxide to support the world's climate change goals.

I would not hesitate to recommend any party interested in looking to start a business opportunity to read the book "Elon Musk by Ashlee Vance." It is a superb read and one that endorses the extraordinary determination and work ethic of Musk. The book by Ashlee Vance in 2015 (updated in 2016) once again reflects and updates what this remarkable man called MUSK has, and continues to achieve and qualifies him (in my mind) as the number one "Entrepreneur" in the world and Mars if his ambition to land their ASAP is achieved! To me, Musk is the "TechnoKing," a name that he has recently adopted with his financial officer at Tesla to be called as "Master of Coin." This supports his two other start-up companies, the brain-reading business "Neuralink" and the tunnel construction group "The Boring Company." He recently declared that he suffers from Asperger's, and having that kind of background, I think people should feel encouraged in accepting Autism in the world we live in, and with some people, and it could turn out to be an advantage, not a disadvantage! Maybe a future US presidential candidate?

Space seems to have an allure for Entrepreneurs besides Elon Musk, with **SpaceX:**

- **Jeff Bezos (Amazon)** with **Blue Origin,** having an idea of developing a space rocket for tourism.
- **Richard Branson** with **Virgin Galactic** working for space travel tourism.
- And **Paul Allen (co-founder of Microsoft)** with **Stratolaunch, a** technology that would send cargo into space.

Jeff Bezos, born in 1964, started Amazon in 1994 out of his garage as an online marketplace for books. In 2018, he was quoted as the richest man in Modern History with a fortune of $150 billion (albeit The Times in 2020 quoted him as worth £200 billion). Not bad from starting as a bookseller!

Bezos will hand over the company's important cloud computing division to Andy Jassy, the boss of Amazon's Web services. Bezos will become executive chairman, a typical Entrepreneurial decision.

The list of Entrepreneurs is endless, and virtually all the products developed were based on a **"Disruptive Business model."**

In other words, the product will only exist if there is an innovative idea behind it that can support its cause. The ability to make people's lives easier at an acceptable cost could form the basis of the Disruptive Business Model. James Dyson should also be recognised as a leading Entrepreneur whose talent was recognised when he developed the Dyson bag less floor cleaner back in 1982, and that was the start of creating a globally recognised Entrepreneur. (See page 76)

My Early Introduction To Business

When I was 13, the youth club that I went to on Saturday evening closed down due to unruly boys causing damage to the hall where music was played, and everybody jived. My friend thought we could easily set up a Saturday teenagers disco at his house as his Mother had previously said he could use the very large area at the top of their house, which was never used. The only problem was that the floor was awful, so we needed Linoleum (Lino) covering. My friend agreed that if I buy the Lino, he will buy the initial cokes, chocolate, crisps, etc., that we would sell to those attending the first night. I used my savings to buy the Lino, with my Mother reluctantly agreeing to me withdrawing my savings and with MOGUS ringing in my ears, **"You are never too young to earn a crust."**

My friend and I carried the substantial roll of Lino from the shop to his house and spent the morning rolling it out on the floor, hopefully ready for the next week's launch. We decided to call the venue "Sherborn Rockers Club" (named after the local Record shop, Sherborn (with soft drinks), where all our friends congregated, drinking milkshakes and chatting up the Girls). We circulated to all our friends the opening day (evening) the following week and that a charge of one shilling per person would be levied.

The grand night arrived, and if my memory serves me correctly, we had about 30 of our friends, boys and girls. I acted as the DJ and my partner as Doorman, Sales, and Cashier (all the money went via him). Halfway through the evening, there was a fight between two boys over a girl, and the main window was smashed, making a substantial noise and glass was strewn outside on the road. His Mother immediately rushed upstairs and told everybody to leave, including me!

I subsequently learned from my partner that his Mother confiscated all the takings plus my Lino as compensation in lieu of replacing the window, cleaning up, and talking to the police when they arrived in response to a neighbour's complaint. What did I learn? My indoctrination as an "Apprentice Entrepreneur" was a disaster and expensive: (MOGUS): **"If only"** – those must be the two saddest words in the world. **If only – what?** If only I had controlled the money and not the disco! (Later in life, I actually registered "If Only. Com".

At 14, I started working as a Saturday salesperson at my Mother's store, where she was a fashion buyer and manager. I served all day on the men's counter for £1. My Mother taught me a great deal as she was a very successful lady in her field. However, a day is a long time standing behind a counter and literally across the department was 'Ladies' fashion' with a number of young Girls of my age also serving as "Saturday hands." Every possible moment I would walk across to chat up the girls, and my Mother used to catch me and made it clear that I was being paid to serve customers, not chat up Girls. The following Saturday, I thought my Mother was away, and once again, I walked over to the Girls and started chatting; my Mother, to my surprise, came out of her office and called me over and into her office. She stated in clear terms, "Kenneth, I have told you on numerous occasions not to go over to the women's department, correct?" "Yes," I said "but..." "But what?" I just shook my head.

"Kenneth, I am dismissing you as from now on you are sacked from this job." I cannot describe my reaction at that time. I just blurted, "but you are my Mother." She replied, "and you were my employee. I want you to leave now." I will remember for the rest of my life my stupid response.

"But I have not yet had lunch!"

"Just go," was the response — my **first sacking, but not the last.**

The second and last sacking was during the early days of my apprenticeship in electrical engineering. It had been a slow couple of days, and Roy Simpson (whom I first met at the company and who went on to become one of my oldest friends and business partners in a company called PEEL) suggested we play the old game of 'knuckles.' Roy had been hitting my knuckles for some time until I managed to get him to miss!

Having built up my anger to hit back, I raised my arm and hit his fist only to hear behind me, "Burgess!!! What do you think you are doing?" It was the foreman.

I barely had time to respond as he then stated: "Burgess, you are suspended for a week. Leave now."

I then responded, "No, you do not have to. I am giving you a weeks' notice."

He responded, **"you don't have to wait a week. You are paid by the hour, so you can leave in an hour!"**

My friend, Roy Simpson, was several years older than me and well into his apprenticeship, which meant he was worth more to the company than myself and was just told to get back to his bench. What did I learn? **(MOGUS.)** *"Operate Brain before opening Mouth."* An extremely important lesson which we all should be wary of.

A quick job to earn money, but how and where?

It was 1961, and I was 18 years old and had recently obtained my driving licence when a friend said, "Ken, a company called Welbeck are looking for drivers for their new concept of a taxi called a "minicab," and they were based in London's Welbeck Street W1." She also stated that I did not need an appointment. I just had to turn up and wait in the Que. I did not know what I was getting into but what a memorable experience it turned out to be. A receptionist met me and told me to join the cue upstairs in the corridor when I got there. I would guess that 99% of the people waiting were 21 and all male. The chat was endless, and everyone asked how your knowledge of London was as you would be asked

16

many questions about both your knowledge of London and how to get from A to B in the shortest possible time! Interestingly, one very bright individual said, let's ask each applicant what the questions were as they leave the room. We asked, and to our surprise, every applicant leaving the room divulged just that, and surprise, surprise, they were all the same questions and supporting correct answers or the corrected answers provided by the person interviewing them.

Therefore, when my turn came, I would "hum and ha" and provide the necessary answer provided by post interviewees, other than one question that I could immediately answer. To cut a long story short, I was given the job as they required many drivers, and I was surprised that they gave you a uniform to wear that was very military-looking and stylish. They also gave training on driving the car and tested your ability, and finally, they provided a two-way telephone wireless radio (NO Wi-Fi in those days). And to my cost, a fare meter!

You were given one free credit in the early days when you had your first fare – Why? When the person got into your cab, you turned the meter on, and when you reached their destination, you turned it off. The number of times that I forgot to turn the meter on, let alone turning it off when arriving at the passenger's destination only to realise that cruising around and waiting for a new fare not realising the on active meter was increasing the cost. It was illegal to pick up a fare unless they had booked by phone to the controller who would then broadcast to drivers as to their current location and the nearest got the fare only to realise that when you had reached the point of collection that you still had your meter on from the previous passenger trip!

You learned quickly.

It was war with the black cab fraternity, something that was growing in violence, and if I remember rightly, some shooting took place, let alone getting false calls for a pick up only to find that when arriving, it was an all-night cafe for Taxi drivers who were ready and waiting with bricks and shovels!

> **(MOGUS):** Success is not final. Failure is non-fatal;
> it is the courage to continue that counts (Winston
> Churchill)

Anyway, my life was moving on, and I made a breakthrough via an invitation to attend an interview at Black and Decker (arranged by my Brother).

Onwards, upwards & even downwards!

My formal business career commenced with Black and Decker (B&D) in 1961, where my older brother worked in marketing & sales. After a year in sales, my brother and I were offered the role by the then General Manager for us to spend a year travelling around the UK, presenting and demonstrating what was to be called the 'B&D Spectacular Road Show.' This was a collapsible stage lighting rigs, sound system etc., and all the furniture and B&D industrial equipment for both displays. We were to demonstrate B&D's industrial equipment to live audiences on a six-day a week basis with all equipment staging etc. moved round the UK, in a substantial Lorry with driver and assistant, to each major town/city throughout the UK to a live commercial audience organised by local B&D management, representatives, and staff.

My brother and I were given what, at that time, was a fantastic financial package. I learned so much about marketing and sales relating to the presentation, organisation, and direct sales approach, all required to make this Marketing & Promotional show a major success – which it was.

Shortly after the road show ended, I moved on to join Ingersoll Rand limited (IR), then, a year later, to Broom and Wade Limited (B&W) – from learning about Electric Tools and Generators to those operated by Pneumatics and Compressed air systems. Again, I met two people who would play a major role in the future development of companies and opportunities, both as partners and shareholders.

1964: Pneumatic Electric Equipment (PEEL). I was working with Broom and Wade when my old friend, Roy Simpson, from apprenticeship days, formed PEEL, with his wife Gloria (whom I introduced Roy to). We kept in close contact for a while, and I introduced the pneumatics side to PEEL. Shortly after, we agreed to develop the company jointly. The company grew, but I was not ready to commit all my other ideas to this venture, and Roy bought my shareholding out, although it was an acrimonious departure. PEEL was a BIG success with ROY and Gloria selling the company several years later.

I had not spoken to Roy for over five years, but our friendship was reinstated years later by what friends have described as *an act of God.*

During my Shanning days, I had to get to a meeting in Los Angeles urgently and the quickest route that day was to fly to San Francisco and take a connection flight to LA. I was flying first class, and when I walked into the first class cabin, there was only one other person in that cabin: Roy Simpson!

We looked at each other and after two minutes of "how are you?" & "Ok, how are you?" we burst into laughter and had one of the funniest and alcoholic flights of my life. When we reached San

Francisco, I had to change terminals and Roy's wife, Gloria, who was already in San Francisco and waiting to meet Roy, was flabbergasted when we both walked into the arrival terminal.

(MOGUS): **"No friendship is an accident."**

1970: Applied Pneumatic Systems Limited (APS Group): After moving on from PEEL, a third party, Gerry Cullimore, an ex-business college from B&W (later joined APS), introduced me to an investment group called Shanning Investment ltd. The group agreed to provide equity investment based on my Business plan to establish a specialist pneumatics company targeting the medical industry and automated production design specifically using 'pneumatic systems engineering' coupled with electronic control systems. During my Broom and Wade days, I learned a great deal about medical compressed air systems and established many clients who used such products.

The automated design side was run by Paul Carter, an ex-friend and colleague from B&W and PEEL who, as an expert in this field, left PEEL to join APS as a director and shareholder.

APS group developed Hospital's central pipe medical gas equipment and controls that were sold globally to major hospital groups and specialist contractors. In addition, APS developed a compressed air 'Jet Engine' starting system in association with Norwegian associates.

APS' success in the development of Pneumatic automated production system for many major companies grew and was highlighted by a one-off. APS was approached by a company called 'Effects Limited' to design and install 'A Rain Maker' for the London Palladium production of 'Singing in the Rain' staring Tommy Steel "singing in the rain" (literally). We did produce it, and it was a big success, thanks to Paul Carter's design skills.

APS packaged Medical Compressed air systems fitted with Mediplex auto control

1974: Carpet – Bagging Globally

My desire to move into other areas associated with the industries that APS was working in enabled me to look at the opportunity to discover the business world beyond the UK via the development of the APS pipe medical gas systems. One of our clients (BOC) invited us to look at a contract they were bidding for in providing the total pipe gas system for a major hospital being constructed in Abu Dhabi. I had never been to the Middle East, in fact, I had never really travelled outside of Europe at that time. Little did I know that it would be a trip that would change my life and business acumen forever! BOC had arranged for their agent to meet me at the arrival airport and take me to the site. My first lesson about Arab traditions and values was at that airport. When I landed and collected my baggage, I waited in the arrival lounge for their agent.

I became restless and kept crossing my legs while sitting down for some time. After five minutes, I could not help noticing that virtually every Arab person who passed by gave me a bad look, and I thought this was not the reception I hoped I may receive. However, when the agent finally turned up, he walked over and, before shaking my hand, he pulled a face and then politely said: "you must never show the sole of your shoe to a passing Arab. "Why?" I asked.

"Showing the sole of your shoe directly in their face means you don't respect them or even care about them. The reference continues with, 'Throw a shoe over them' – meaning, they are like dirt that you don't

even respect them by hitting them with your hand. Since the sole of the shoe is the one place that addresses dirt which means anyone facing that sole is equal to the sole of your shoe!"

I apologized this was the first of many lessons learned about Culture, be it Arabic, Chinese, African, Indian, Russian and all the other countries in Europe and the world. Was it an important lesson? More than you will ever believe and the first of many that I had to understand as my role was to sell my company's brand, its products, and confidence in its managing director, Ken Burgess.

"Cultural differences affect both Marketing and trading behaviours. Culture will always influence trading, as the inherent characteristics of a nation will always impact behaviour of all kinds, whether social, personal or financial."

– 'The Times' Raconteur supplement

It was important to understand specific and frequently used key phrases in Arabic; my Arabic business friends said first and arguably the most important words which are used 24 hours per day – **"Inshallah" – God Willing** followed by: **"Buckram" – Tomorrow;** and "Maalesh" – **Never-mind/Does not matter.**

Little did I know that the visit to the hospital construction site would also play a major role in the development of both existing and new companies. I was shown around the various areas and the questionable problems related to available space at the site.

However, I assured the representative that APS could provide the equipment and installation required within a very quick time period. Looking around the construction, I noticed hundreds of boxes of all shapes and sizes stacked around the construction site. I asked why and what were they doing on-site. The response was that the contract to equip the hospital is a total-turkey contract provided by one company. They provide, install and commission everything that goes into a hospital: medical, furniture, kitchens, workshops, radiology, commercial offices, even down to the knives and forks. He said that only one company in the world can do this and quoted a specific company. I did not realize that they would subsequently become a true competitor for many years to come.

In speaking to the general manager of the group responsible for the hospital being developed, I asked why the products that are being supplied under the contract seem to have all been stored together and not phased for delivery and installation and, in my mind, subject to damage, theft etc. when not distributed to the sight against a set program? He agreed and said that they would have preferred a phased delivery program and asked if we were aware of any company who, at that time, could do this. I responded with, "yes, one of my companies. Why do you ask?" He replied, "we have a second hospital project which is an expansion of an existing hospital. Would you like to consider tendering for the total equipping contract?" I said yes, and he asked for the company's details and then he would provide me with the tender schedule!

I hesitated and stuttered saying, "Shanning" to which he said, just Shanning? I stuttered again and said off the top of my head Shanning International limited at the same address as APS.

Shanning was the investment company that had invested in APS. Ron Botting, the main partner of Shanning Investment, later joined Shanning International as Chairman/Financial Director. Ron was a qualified FCA and his experience and full-time involvement in Shanning was immense. Shanning International started a new global company and eventually a group holding company called Shanning Group Limited.

However, time was not on our side, and we had little to no knowledge on the product and/or the manufacturers to equip a hospital, but obviously, we knew how to plan, install and commission.

(MOGUS): "Imagination more important than knowledge." (Einstein)

When I returned to the UK, I immediately contacted a friend of mine whom I had known for many years, she was a Theatre Sister. I explained my predicament and although I had a Schedule of all equipment required for the hospital, we required information and lots of it!

Together with some of my team, we worked 12 hours a day over the weekend to establish everything we needed to address the manufacturer's names and technical specifications, etc. Within two weeks, we had enough information to complete a detailed

"Turnkey Quotation" for the project's supply, installation, and commissioning. And of course, a total turnkey price in one currency – Sterling, albeit that we purchased product, internationally, in as many as five different currencies. After several meetings, both in Abu Dhabi and the UK, Shanning International was awarded the contract which we successfully completed some nine months later.

The Group's key companies coupled with new projects/developments ranged over 30 years, with the main exception being my holding company, Visual Investments International Limited, (VIIL) which I set up in 1980 to specialize in investment and research. VIIL is still active some 40 plus years later, with shareholders being my Sons and Athena Wan, my long-standing accountant and friend of many years. I am not addressing in detail the numerous other company start-ups and/or investments made by VIIL, some successful and some not so successful.

Key Corporate developments

1970: Applied Pneumatics Limited

1975+: Shanning International Limited/Shanning Group Limited

Middle East Magic with healthcare projects awarded in: UAE, Egypt, Oman, Saudi Arabia, Iraq, Libya, followed by India, Malaysia, and China.

1976+: Nigerian chaos and all that the business entails. Endorsing western business ethics might make you sleep better at night, but it will not necessarily enable you to win the contract, let alone complete them. Shanning won the first contract in June 1979 to equip 256 Health Centres throughout Nigeria.

1980 – 2021+: Visual Investments International Limited (VIIL) is a holding company owned by myself, my sons, and our accountant. It was established in January 1980, and 40+ years later, it is still active in exploring, researching, and developing new opportunities.

1980: Forward Health Limited, the first Sports Injury treatment clinic encompassing osteopathy, naturopathy, and conventional health treatment.

1984: Shanning Pod Limited, related to Design & Development of a 'Demountable Mobile Healthcare product.'

1984: International Care Services Limited (ICS), JV with Extendicare of Canada (Crown Life) Nursing homes & Hospitals own and manage. Extendicare was a very well-established nursing home group in Canada with an established reputation for quality. The brand name we established for the nursing home group was *Rosecrest Care Homes*, the first custom-built home for 53 residents which was opened in 1988 at Ash-Hurst Park in Kent. In 1992, ICS was sold to its joint venture partners.

1984: East West East Limited, Hong Kong and China-based for Health,

Leisure & Sporting projects, specifically post-Olympics, the first commercial event in association with our JV partners (International Media Productions) at the Birds Nest Stadium "The Race of Champions."

1988: Shanning Laser Systems, JV with partner Dr. Mark Clement and his team from Swansea University.

1991: Shanning Mobility Systems Limited. The mobility company was acquired by Shanning and changed its name to the aforementioned. The company had developed a range of very special market-led products targeting the disabled and obese with chairs that helped them to move around with ease. Furthermore, they had addressed the problem of the inflexibility of battery-driven invalid chairs with an all-terrain four-wheel drive.

This design had great potential, but we did not have the expertise in power-driven vehicles. Therefore, we contacted Frank Williams, CEO of Williams cars, for two reasons. One, he used an electric wheelchair, and two, Williams was (and still is) a very entrepreneurial engineering company. We asked if his company would be interested in working with us on this exciting four-wheel-drive wheelchair. However, Frank Williams wrote back, politely declining.

1994: Eye Academy Limited established the first day centres (London & Birmingham) in Europe to specifically provide LASIC – Laser Refractive Surgical Correction.

1998: SpaceFM limited. This was one of the first dance music, online radio stations, set up by my sons, who kindly invited their father to participate with them. A whole new world of language, ethics, and improvisation with the first "Shed-built" sound studio was achieved with great success until 911, which had a very marked effect on contracts under negotiation with a number of major airlines to encompass Space FM in their in-flight entertainment. Space FM ceased operation sometime later.

Shanning International Limited and Shanning Group Ltd became the UK leaders in the total hospital concept, medical laser technology, and nursing homes. Shanning International Limited carried out contracts exceeding $110,000.000 during its seventeen years of exports worldwide.

Shanning International limited went on to complete some 220 medical-related projects in 22 countries over a 17 year period and was awarded, amongst others, The Sunday Times award for Enterprising Britain (1980); the Queen's Award for Export Achievement (1981), and Shanning Laser Systems, in association with its partner Dr. Mark Clement, won the Welsh Design technology award for the Sirius 300 Laser in 1988.

1988 Promotional launch of Shanning Group with UK minister, as guest, with Ken Burgess.

Current projects and developments

Established January 1980, Visual Investments International Limited holding company and research / investment.

2008 – 2014 onwards: Livetime2 Limited. Research and development of stand-alone Mobile broadcasting unit.

2012 – 2021 onwards: Broadcasting Investments Group Limited (BIG), currently (2021) investment via VIIL into BANTA, Simple stream, TV Player. LT2

1980: Forward Health, JV with Terry Maule (Osteopath/Naturopath), the first of its kind to combine conventional and alternative medicine in the treatment of sports injuries, fitness, and wellbeing whilst addressing the desires and demands of Roger Utley, Seb Coe, Gerry Francis, to name but a few patients. Roger Utley joined the company shortly afterwards.

SUPER SEB IN TOWN

THE MOST famous man in the world today visited Hemel Hempstead, this week.

Sebastian Coe, triple world record holder in the 800m, 1500m and the mile, was the special guest at the opening of Forward House, in St. John's Road, Boxmoor, Hemel Hempstead, the health clinic branch of Forward Health Ltd., on Wednesday.

The brilliant Coe had nothing but praise for the clinic and the man who will run the enterprise, Terry Moule, the director of therapeutics.

Seb said: "Last winter I was troubled with a back problem, but within a couple of visits to Terry, I was running again, and I am extremely grateful to him. I think this is a marvellous place and I am sure it will succeed."

The whole idea of Forward Health has arisen from the principle of naturopathy — the theory that it is more important to create health than to treat disease and that health is down to the responsibility of the individual. They must be aware of their own body and take a positive approach to realise fitness, be they trained athletes or the man in the street.

Former England rugby captain, Roger Uttley, general manager and physical educationalist at Forward House, is another sportsman who benefited from the treatment of Terry Moule, returning to play full-time first-class rugby after serious injury had threatened his career.

Footballer, Gerry Francis, ex-England captain and now with Crystal Palace, is another famous sportsman who has resumed his career at the top following advice and treatment from Mr. Moule.

The fully-trained staff at Forward House are there to treat people in the correct training and maintaining of their fitness. Their interest is in the health and well-being of the individual.

● Pictured (left to right), Terry Moule, Sebastian Coe and Roger Uttley.

(MOGUS): *"We are what we eat, what we drink, what we breathe, and what we think."*

1984: Shanning POD Limited, the first demountable mobile health care facility of its kind in the world. I was travelling in our agents' car to the airport in Saudi Arabia when we passed several damaged mobile healthcare units on the side of the road. Minutes later, we passed several others parked on a trailer. When I commented on the spectacle, my agent stated that it was common because of the accidents and mechanical problems, which meant that many mobile healthcare and X-ray units were unable to be used due to vehicle problems and not the facilities within them. All the way back to the UK, I kept thinking about how can we address this problem, why can the equipment, etc., not be encompassed within a demountable unit. That evening at home and prior to my getting back to the office in the morning, I was served beans in a pod with my salad. I immediately saw a pea inside a pod!!!!! I gathered our team together in the morning and explained my observations about mobile healthcare systems and the POD option. It was met by a lot of enthusiasm, but first, we needed to review the market for possible alternatives that would meet the criteria.

Nine months later, the team, in collaboration with a manufacturer of large fiberglass vessels, had designed the first prototype. We decided that we would use a four-wheel all-terrain vehicle for POD to travel on, which was a Landover. The rest is history. It was a great success with orders from Japan, China, South Africa, Indonesia, and Saudi Arabia.

Post our release of the POD Radiology unit, a request was received from Sheikh Mohamed Maktoum, one of the world's leading racehorse owners. They wanted to know if our unit could provide an X-ray POD for use on his camels. Now, how do you get a racing camel into a POD? The answer is with difficulty. Obviously, camels would not fit into a POD, much to the Sheikh's disdain, but we satisfied him by saying that the X-ray head in POD was designed to be fixed or mobile, enabling radiology procedures to be taken to the patient, or in his situation, to the Camel. Finally, Sheikh Mohamed ended up buying an x-ray Pod.

The POD's total development cost was recouped by 1987. POD brand name was sold in later years to Ford Motor Company and the Pod design concept to a South African company under license.

POD on Land Rover

Sales were made to China, Japan, South Africa, the Middle East, and Africa.

China 1984. A whole new meaning in doing business the Chinese way means that "saving face" can make or break a deal. Eating at your host's banquet becomes a whole new experience, and a simple translation of both the spoken and written word can test the patience of a saint – for both sides!

Sport, Sport, and more Sport: Redeveloping an old investment into (hopefully) a leading Chinese/European Sport and Media agency and being faced with the trials and tribulations of sports stars and teams such as KaKa, Bolt, and AC Milan or do I mean their management!

A major feasibility Study for a Health and Leisure complex encompassing Hospital, Nursing Home, Hotel, Sports development clinic, Housing within a major 27 whole Golf development in Shenzhen, was prepared by Shanning in **1985. Only to be advised by our JV partner at the final stage of agreement that "by the way, the land is a burial ground, and we have to negotiate with every representative of each person buried there to purchase their rights." Needless to say, it would have been impossible to make the project pay on those terms.**

2009: Surprise, surprise! When finalizing the first (post-Olympic) commercial event at the iconic Birds Nest stadium in Beijing, we found that the centre of the playing area had a substantial gaping hole that accommodated a lift. Not the best discovery when we were planning to hold a football match on it! However, after this problem was corrected and carried out the match successfully, we were allowed to follow up with the introduction and promotion of the "Race of Champions" with many Formula-1 drivers taking part. This event was in association with International Media Productions, the founders of "Race of Champions" established in 1988 with productions in over 100 countries.

1988: Shanning Laser Systems Limited.

Shanning International Limited in association with its JV partners from Swansea University led by Dr Mark Clement won the Welsh Design Technology award for the Shanning portable Sirius 300 Laser.

Established in association with Dr Mark Clement and his three-man team at the Innovation Centre, Swansea University College. The product was a range of lightweight carbon dioxide medical laser instrument generating huge interest from both Europe and the USA. The company was eventually sold to Dr Clement in 1990.

Shanning Sirius 300 Laser

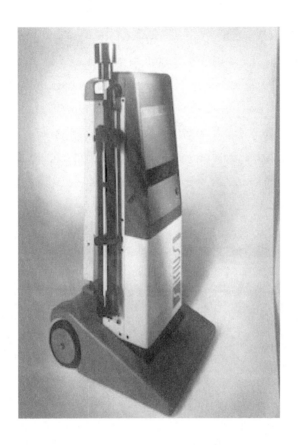

1990: Health and Leisure International Limited (HLI).
Developing Collingtree Park, the first signature (Johnny Miller)
golf course, in the UK, designed to US.

PGA standards were set within the first, comprehensive Golf,
Residential, Health-Care, Nursing Home and Teaching

Academy. In addition, HLI pioneered Cayman Golf, the short ball concept developed by Jack Nicklaus IE 'Cayman Golf.'

Why did we wish to get involved in golf? A golf course development takes up a substantial amount of land, and, as a standalone development, it is not the most profitable but conducive to associated developments which make such a project financially very viable such as: housing, hotel, sports medicine, care homes, to name but a few. I was introduced to the phrase relating to Housing as being "productive landscaping" beneficial to both residential owners and developers alike.

HLI sold its investment to Gamalstarden Bank in 1993.

"Developing Collingtree Park – Golf Course"

1994: The Eye Academy Limited

Pioneering in the UK's first commercial Laser Refractive Surgery, the "LASIK" (Laser Assisted in Situ KeratomLeusis) way. Ethics, Egos and Entrepreneurial Surgeons: nothing changes. We developed Centres in Birmingham followed by Harley Street in London. The company was eventually sold in 1999 to Canadian public company, Icon Inc.

BIRMINGHAM LAUNCH OF EYE LASER ACADEMY

The Eye Academy, Harley Street London

"Laser treatment room"

Ken Burgess

2008: Livetime2 limited (LT2), arguably the greatest opportunity at that time for a truly unique global communications product that took some six years of development. A contract placed with a third party contractor in 2012 to complete software development created mayhem which some years later is still being legally addressed via our holding companies, VIIL and BIG.

LT2 mobile operator demonstrating

The chaos of global marketing, selling and negotiating in developed and developing countries, supported or otherwise!

There are variable degrees of UK government co-operation, coupled with the different interpretations experienced from commercial departments at UK embassies as opposed to that of other European and US embassies! What do I mean by this in the early days is that the feedback and commercial intelligence was not as forthcoming as what the French and US embassies were capable of.

However, when Margaret Thatcher came to power, in 1979, things started to change and exporters, like Shanning, started to obtain very good briefings and co-operation from the commercial side of the embassies.

There are Arabs and Arabs and then there are the Lebanese and the Egyptians. I had to learn quickly in order to understand their differences, idiosyncrasies and above all that old Arab saying that goes, "I against my Brother, My Brother and I against my Cousin and all of us against our enemy!" This was very evident when we started to negotiate our first major contract in Egypt for the first private hospital project since Nasser came to power. The Al - Salaam Hospital, in Cairo, was the brain child of Dr Mohamed Magdi. After many meetings in both Egypt and back in the UK with Dr Magdi, we were advised that the architects for the hospital design were American and that they had requested that a French company had also been invited to tender and that the MD for the hospital, Dr Mohamed Magdi, would be finalising the contract for the Total Equipping in New York on a specific day. The French were favourites to be awarded the contract primarily due to the financial package being better than the one we were offering with ECGD funding against the French equivalent. Dr Magdi advised us that the French team would be arriving the following day in NY with the intention of signing the contract. The agent for the French company was, we were advised, a Lebanese, whereas, we had retained an Egyptian agent!

The race began, in a BA Concorde, across the Atlantic, against a French competitor in an Air France Concorde.

The prize?

Egypt's largest private health care project – the Al Salaam Hospital.

The French Concorde was delayed, giving me an hour to persuade the Chairman, Dr Mohamed Magdi, of the Egyptian group, who at that time was in discussions with their US architects in New York – "The benefits of buying British." We were successful and accordingly became a cause of much dissatisfaction of the French group as some weeks later at Shanning's offices, Dr Magdi signed the contract with the English company, Shanning International.

(MOGUS): *It's never over until the fat lady starts to sing"* ... *(I cannot remember ever seeing the "fat lady!")*

Cutting a deal in India with the UK's Hinduja brothers (2nd richest persons in the UK and 49th in the world, as per Sunday Times' Rich list of 2020) taught me that charity and loyalty do not necessarily go hand in hand. The Brothers were a delight to work with and their generosity both in the UK and India was very special. We carried out a consultancy contract regarding their Hinduja National Hospital project in India with the view to negotiate the equipping and commissioning. Unfortunately, a key long term employee who was responsible for overseeing the project inferred that the second phase would not be going ahead. I still wear the 'Hinduja' watch that the Brothers gave me as a gift.

Then I observed Prime Minister Thatcher's caring side at number 10 change to her business woman side at Chequers. Did I find politics and business to mix together and if so, at what price? Mrs Thatcher was a very keen supporter of Entrepreneurism as supporting start-ups was a big part of her free market agenda. Businessman, Sir John Harvey Jones, who fronted the BBC's Troubleshooter series on small firms believed that Thatcher helped to create a golden age for entrepreneurship. Thatcher's reforms were designed to make it easier to set up and run a business.

I first met Mrs Thatcher during a business reception at number 10. During our conversation, a waitress dropped a tray stacked with glasses very near to us. Despite a rush of aids, Thatcher was the first person to help the young woman pick up broken glass and saying, "don't worry, it is not a problem, go and get yourself sorted out and come back when you feel able." We resumed our conversation with her comment "we all make errors, me included!"

I was invited to attend a whole day's meeting at the Prime ministers formal country residence – 'Chequers.' The meeting was with other key health care industry representatives and key ministers. The PM certainly led that day in a very positive and constructive manner and made no bones about it. "The Lady was not for turning" and if there was any point which she was unsure about, she requested a more detailed explanation before moving on.

Awards and more awards: Did they produce investment opportunities and government support?

1980: Ken Burgess: Sunday Times award for Enterprising Britain & the *start of an export boom?*

1981: Shanning International Limited: Winners of The Queens Awards for Export Achievement (*more business lunches?*)

1988: Shanning Laser Limited: The Welsh National Business Awards. *Recognition relating to the success of design team at Swansea University.*

1988: POD Limited: Design Council Award, for Innovation and Technology for POD mobiles. Global interest and an enquiry for use with a camel.

1990: Shanning Lasers Limited: Runner up in Prince of Wales – BBC's Tomorrows World for Technology Innovation. Sparked lots of media interest.

My Iraq apocalypse:

Shanning International's demise in 1990:

The two faces of the DTI, Bank of England, the politics of the day paired with the indecisiveness of the UK government, and the let down with turmoil and indecision at the banks was enough to make any hardened entrepreneur question the values of pursuing international bonded contracts. The UK government of the day implemented a Trade Embargo which stopped all exports to Iraq, including health related contracts.

Even more critical was the situation when your bank removes from your account all funds (current and deposit), without notice, to pay out a multimillion pound on-demand performance bond called by Rasheed bank on behalf of your client in Iraq during the Iraqi/Kuwait war! This act not only stopped my company Shanning International from both pursuing let alone completing its hospital projects in Baghdad. This was contrary to the recommendations made by the United Nations that health related projects should be allowed to continue providing they were not military-related. Despite substantial lobbying, the only feedback was that the government had been advised that some of the medical equipment due to be shipped had military implications. Despite such an absurd statement, the government refused to provide any information relating to their claim.

The legal battle was extensive in both time and money and ended up with my company having to go into administration with loss of Millions of pounds. Our Iraq offices, workshop, equipment and vehicles were lost plus equipment was paid for and unable to be shipped out. In 2001, a decade later, the banks (Lloyds and Rasheed (*See Goggle/HOL Shanning International*) lost their appeal in the House of Lords and Shanning's administrators won the case. All a bit late to save the company, its employees and investors. This act had a major knock-on effect for Shanning Group Limited.

Consider A Business Partnership?

What makes a good partnership?

I have found a golden rule which says that each partner must bring something different to the business. For example, Financial, Sales and/or Marketing, Engineering/Manufacturing (if relevant), Commercial aspect. The legal aspect is also interesting but not a requirement unless the product reflects substantial legal input or control. But it is not of great advantage in a small company start-up.

Many of the sports agencies and player management organisations were founded by lawyers. One of the most successful, IMG, was the creation of the highly successful, the late, Mark McCormack, pioneer, guru and entrepreneur in sport management, representation, film and television production. His first book, *"What they don't teach you at Harvard Business School"* is a must-read for any individual starting in business, especially those MBA graduates.

If your partner or partners bring a diversification of skills and/or experience, then you are on the right track, otherwise, if you all have the same skills and experience, it may be a recipe for disaster.

(MOGUS): **"Too many cooks spoil the broth."**

Next comes the emotive subject as to who heads up the business. Do I hear, *"we feel that it would be right to have joint Co-Founder title"*? Yes, but Chief Executive? Don't do it as it will be a disaster. Before anyone quotes examples of successful joint MD/CEO of specific companies, I would say they are not the norm. Investors are not happy with that structure and I have only seen disasters as a result of joint MD/CEO's with companies being pulled apart. Who then takes the position? It does not necessarily have to be the founder, or the prime funding source (*it's my money so I will be CEO*) or the entrepreneur.

It is my experience that you can have a Chairperson with experience, part or full-time, thereby enabling the founder to take up the role of CEO, enabling the chairperson to guide and assist in the development of the CEO and company. This provides considerable benefits to 'all and sundry,' especially investors.

It is interesting that Elon Musk who held the positions of Chairman and CEO recently changed to CEO and established a separate Chairperson of Tesla.

One should also bear in mind the quote, not, I hasten to-say from my old granny, but this time from Einstein, who stated and I quote:

"Imagination is more important than "Knowledge" – or should it be the Entrepreneur!

The MD/CEO has to be a good communicator, determined, numerate and prepared to take on most tasks if required, including cleaning the toilets and above all he or she must be a good listener, who leads by example. In a start-up, cash prudence can make or break the start-up company. (The failing of many a dot com company). I am reminded however of (MOGUS), *"Penny wise and Pound foolish."*

A contradiction? No, it means keeping expenditure to a minimum within the workforce and working environment, with little control on director's expenditure, facilities and perks! Alternatively, showing the same tight financial controls and disciplines relating to contractual expenditure, that you require from operational costs.

New business start-ups at 60 plus! – Social TV for all!

Age is no barrier to a challenge, only money, energy and integrity! The evidence that older people are, if anything, becoming more enterprising should help to calm two of the biggest worries. One is that the greying of the population will inevitably produce economic sluggishness. The second is that older people will face hard times as companies shed older workers in the name of efficiency and the welfare states cut back on their pensions.

According to the Office of National Statistics in the UK, there are more than 13,000 companies being formed every week compared with 11,000 during the same period last year, in 2019. Now is the time to launch your idea, remember?

(MOGUS), "He (or she) who hesitates is lost."

Research suggests that age may, in fact, be an advantage for entrepreneurs. It is my opinion that during and post the end to 'COVID 19,' there will never be a more innovative, opportunistic and creative environment for starting a business since the industrial revolution. However, the one factor that has emerged during the Covid 19 period is the stress and strain experienced by key workers and management at all levels, during, and without doubt, post the pandemic has and will continue to have an impact on their mental health and wellbeing. Hence, support from all the management team and investors must be mandatory if the company is to succeed. I would quote a recent statement by Entrepreneur Guy Tolhust: *Pressures have grown on founders. The expectations are not just that you are good at running a business – you have to be a good figurehead, a good spokesperson, a good investor, liaison, press-ready, and able to take on HR responsibilities.*

New and improved technology introduces new opportunities

The GIG Economy of changing attitudes, standards and preferences and reliance on freelances, independent workers, part-time and temporary, will grow rapidly, especially true for the online GIG economy. There are still a lot of investment funds available for the right product and they are growing even more for the "GIG" **Entrepreneur. You can call these one-off jobs on a casual basis.**

Compared to 5 years ago, the technology/products enabling one to market and sell locally, nationally and internationally, via the Internet and social media, has increased substantially as has research with the likes of Internet search engines that bring a whole new meaning to research. Moreover, since COVID19 introduces the new home-office marketer with the opportunity to both market and sell on line, which is really beneficial for both abled and disabled home-workers, and when coupled with flexible working time, the whole arrangement provides new found benefits for all – regardless of gender.

The concept of an APP was virtually unheard of before 2007. Growth in manufacturing is now an obvious factor of many an APP success encouraged by what one would define as the NORM in marketing of APPvertising! "App Annie" sets the total number of apps downloaded in 2020 at 130 billion, up by 10% from the previous year.

The Cloud and 5G

In my opinion, the two most influential and beneficial things to do, especially for start-up but also for the established enterprises, is migrating to the cloud, particularly when developing in a new country as it illuminates the need for new data centres and requirement to install new servers. As an example, the Amazon Web Services Cloud (AWS) is specifically designed to host large-scale international operations.

Cloud computing enables businesses of all sizes to generate more revenue with reduced costs and increased efficiency. It is also green, enabling companies to reduce their carbon footprint when utilising AWS. I was encouraged when being advised that 200,000 tons of CO_2 emissions are saved each year by UK clients of AWS alone – the equivalent of 400 million trees. When expanding into new countries, the need to find new data centres and install new servers becomes a "thing of the past" as Cloud reduces the cost of exporting/operating in new countries when using AWS and, at the same time, increasing the efficiency of the in-company operations.
(Ref: awsimpactreport)

The introduction of **5G** can and will provide ideas and substantial benefits to almost all companies but specifically when connection speeds are estimated to be between 10 and 100 hundred times faster than 4G but also more data can be transmitted across the network with minimal delay. In turn, it becomes feasible to move substantially more of the processing that one would be using individual devices into the Cloud providing additional benefits relating to applications and digital experiences; an example benefiting: Healthcare, Retail, and Entertainment to name but a few sectors.

Where will 5G have the biggest impact? Using figures produced by Cisco 2020, 5G will cause the most disruption in the sectors of:

1. **Automotive 70%.**
2. **Cloud Services 57%.**
3. **Manufacturing 35%.**
4. **Retail 27%.**
5. **Logistics and transportation 27%.**
6. **Online gaming and video 24%.**
7. **Healthcare 20%.**
8. **Energy 13%.**

Entertainment (Internet) is arguably one, if not the biggest, gains during COVID 19 with all aspects of entertainment now being developed for home entertainment, the likes of what we have not seen before. Couple this with the development and expansion of the home office and it's acceptability as the "**Satellite Office**" or **offices** of that business, and you get a pretty disruptive picture.

I have tried in this book to share with the reader my experience and expertise after a lifetime in the heady world of entrepreneurial business development.   The book has an account of all my successes, failures and provides advice on the delicate art of negotiation by taking the reader through the rules of engagement when closing a deal, and much, much more.

So if the party already has those natural entrepreneurial skills, the passion to win, and equally as important, – a sense of humour **(MOGUS)** *"No Humour, No heart",* then this book could be the tool that will unlock those negative thoughts and hone the positive ones. If not, whatever the level of one's ambition – it will certainly help understand the trials and tribulations when first evaluating if their idea for a business or product is viable, prior to starting on the road to even greater success for their own business or businesses!

Starting a new business doesn't have an age-cap. You can start it whether you are 11 (never to early) or to the contrary 60+ (it's never too late). After all, it is businessman Warren Buffet (Berkshire Hathaway) who said, in 2019, "I have more fun than I think any 88 year old is having anywhere" and he is still active in developing new investments. In fact, Warren bought his first shares in 1942 aged 11. Making money in today's markets using online promotion and sales in an entrepreneurial manner can mean buying and selling or even promoting, just ask the 11 year old in the US, **Kheris Rogers,** who in 2017, became the youngest ever designer to present a line at New York fashion week.

True Entrepreneurs given the right opportunities, hands-on support and guidance can, and invariably do, fine-tune those basic instincts to a point of perfection or as (MOGUS) would say, *"Experience cannot be bought and cannot be taught."*

Am I Entrepreneurial?

Developing a business from scratch and maintaining that business is within the realms of many people, given there is an appropriate proportion of enthusiasm, desire, passion, support and of course money! The very nature of being entrepreneurial exposes you to a whole raft of nail-biting, heart-stopping, life-changing, soaring highs and desperate lows kind of experiences and situations. You don't have to be a genius to succeed unless genius is reflected.

(MOGUS): *"Genius is 99% perspiration and 1% inspiration. (Thomas Edison)*

For good or for bad, I have experienced them all, and I will share my experiences with you.

Do Men make better Entrepreneurs than Women?

In my view, invariably yes, but are there exceptions? Yes! There are. I believe there are inherent reasons for this as generally men are greater risk-takers than women but women compared to men do have some special traits when it comes to evaluating situations, specifically 'intuition' that I believe is well developed in the female species! I have lost count during my life when in the company of women (either at a party, reception, and or, meeting), I have made positive comments about somebody we had been introduced to only to be challenged by my female companion with views to the contrary which in many cases their judgement has been proven correct. To the contrary, however, I have found so many women very cautious about taking a risk or being indecisive about committing to an investment. In some cases, they were right to be cautious.

(MOGUS): *"The Policy of being too cautious is the greatest risk of all." (NEHRU)*

Starting a business!

Many of the problems experienced in the course of developing a business, whether it is a local business or one that has grown into an internationally accepted brand, can have a common link. I will cover initial feasibility (seed) to start-up and then on to early stage; marketing, sales, production, financial and legal matters. From the smallest start-up to the group operation, I have been directly involved in the day-to-day operation and development of dozens of start-up companies and will share my experience with the reader that amongst all the requirements and understanding, Integrity plays a very important part, especially when the Entrepreneur brings in new equity investment, i.e. **Shareholder(s) and all which that entails!**

How important is being market-led as opposed to product-led?

The first and potentially the costliest lesson that every start-up must address is the importance of understanding that being **market-led** as opposed to **product-led** is the only option available. This is covered in greater detail in 'Feasibility/Research' section.

Don't get carried away with romantic dreams, unproven and unsubstantiated ideas. Companies House is full of derelict companies and banks with worthless guarantees, unless of course the bank has got you to pledge your home as a guarantee!

Proper business accountancy, corporate governance practices, advice and support is mandatory for all companies regardless of their size. The start-ups, arguably, are one of the most abused by the majority of seed, start-up and even early stage companies or should I say the Founder/CEO/ & Entrepreneur. Having a good accountancy practice will support your business from day one.

To ignore sound business accountancy advise and practice can, and will inevitably, lead to delays, increased costs and frustration from potential investors and shareholders alike that in many cases lead to even bigger disasters where the only parties to benefit are the lawyers and in certain circumstances **'The Founder(s)!'**

Pneumatic Engineering, Healthcare, Medical Technology, Recreational Sport, Information Technology and, last but not least, Broadcasting are all business sectors with which I have personally been associated and referred to in this book. And when it comes to many other business challenges encountered by budding Entrepreneurs and/or businesspersons during the course of developing a business, I have placed special emphasis upon dealing with Partnerships, be they social, business or family. All of them are prone to be problematic unless due consideration is addressed, regularly!

There are pitfalls to be aware of when forming/establishing a business relationship. 24x365 =????? Hours in a year? Maybe, but also the number of hours you will live, eat and sleep when starting and running a business.

(MOGUS) would say, *"Don't fall in love with the business, fall in love with the balance sheet."* Unfortunately, I did not practice what MOGUS preached, I fell in love with a business and the knock-on effect was disastrous. Leave emotional attachments to family, pets and old Entrepreneurs. A business is an asset (hopefully) and like all assets there comes a time to sell and realise a profit. What value do you put on a company's brand and/or its intellectual property?

Money, money, money makes the world go round. It also comes at a price – be it for equity investment, working capital, project finance or bridging poor cash flows, all speak a common language in the business arena.

Let's talk about the pitfalls and adventures of Carpet bagging when negotiating with government related contracts in both developing and developed countries. The bigger the contract value, the greater potential for bribery and corruption, sorry I should say, 'Commissions/Expenses' which are potentially experienced at most levels and stages. There are no holds barred in the pursuance of International business. Conducting business in developing countries is difficult enough without the so-called well-meaning concerns of individuals in the public eye! Debt release and aid will in many cases not directly help cure the problems experienced by developing, and in some cases, developed countries when it comes to improving the quality of everyday life for the overwhelming majority of that population. My views are based on fact & not rhetoric.

Bonds (Performance and Tender) & the scourge of any new, and in some cases, established businesses with a contracting arm. My Company was held to ransom by George Wimpy relating to a project in Oman – now you see it, now you don't. This is the tale of a performance bond (£600,000) and the untold damage it can do to a company when used as an instrument of persuasion, & or, words to that effect. However, after that, event we received apologies from Wimpy, in writing, with a total refund of all payments made including costs.

The million pound plus Bond called by Llyods bank during the Iraq invasion of Kuwait, confiscation of all equipment waiting installation in our office in Iraq demolished with all assets removed including vehicles, UK government's refusal to allow Shanning to complete its contract in allowing it to ship out all medical equipment to Iraq (Internationally agreed by UN) in order to complete the project had a devastating effect to the Group's major company, Shanning International. The effect was so disastrous that after seventeen successful trading years, the Directors were left with no alternative but to place the company in liquidation. In turn, this had a knock-on effect to the group's holding company. This is a story in its own right of intrigue, government indifference and bankers' incompetence which, several years later, was eventually corrected when Llyods lost the appeal made via the liquidators of Shanning (*Look on Google – Shanning International Vs Lloyds – International/UK court of appeal*).

What are the risks in a personal guarantee? Answer: Everything down to your cufflinks. That answer came from an experience when I became an underwriting name at Lloyds of London (founded in 1686). I learned a life changing lesson when, in 1970, a fraud cost me dearly because I had no understanding of the potential dangers and pitfalls when providing Personal Guarantees with absolutely no control on the investments that I was guaranteeing! Not something you would wish to experience when investing in a business. I should have taken heed and read, **not MOGUS, but the late John F Kennedy's statement:** *"How could I have been so mistaken as to have trusted the experts?"*

What makes a successful Entrepreneur?

If one knew the precise formula, they could make a fortune. It is my opinion that you cannot teach people to become Entrepreneurial, the same as you cannot teach a person to sell or to act. They either have it in their character and personality or they do not – there is no halfway. Of course, you can, and invariably will, develop and improve their skills as well as enhance thinking, hunger and desire to succeed which are all part of an Entrepreneur's personality; and mandatory too if they want to win, or for the more conservative, **"succeed in life."** The entrepreneur enjoys the challenge of developing new, innovative ideas into a successful product, business and brand. They are genuine creators of wealth. They are the men and women who, in many cases, are prepared to risk everything in the pursuit of success. I believe that simply developing a successful business does not necessarily make that person an Entrepreneur – although they may be a successful businessperson. So what do I believe are the major differences between the two?

'Entrepreneurism' is akin to having an addiction. The fix comes from developing an idea to a point where it is proven, established, and hopefully in a position to exit profitably. However, there is always the possibility of failure, a word not in the dictionary of any self-respecting Entrepreneur.

You can make a businessperson, given that they are ambitious, but it is my belief that you cannot make an entrepreneur as they are born with the type of personality, drive and impatience that is intrinsic only to the entrepreneur. To clarify what I mean by being born with the relevant attributes, I quote from a very successful and true entrepreneur, Sir James Goldsmith, who is sadly no longer with us, but to me, he epitomised the word entrepreneur and all it stands for and his definition of an entrepreneur was:

"Entrepreneurs come in all shapes and sizes, the common theme that links them is sound judgement, ambition, determination, capacity to asses and to take risks, hard work, greed, fear and luck. On the whole, entrepreneurs are uneducated or self-educated. Our western education produces specialists whereas entrepreneurs must be generalists." – **Sir James Goldsmith.**

I was fortunate to meet him or should I say, bump into him, in the gents at number 10 Downing Street, as dinner guests of the then prime minister Margaret Thatcher. I noticed that he was 'ambidextrous' as he had perfected the knack of holding his ever present cigar during every eventuality! **A true entrepreneur**.

In examining Sir James's views, I would add three further requirements: **Inspiration**, the ability to inspire others even when the going gets difficult and at times, downright impossible. I would then always consider **Stoic**, that if it were easy, everybody would be doing it – a tenacious streak to win. However, and above all, 'a **sense of humour.'**

I was also fortunate enough to meet a very successful self-made Canadian entrepreneur and author, G. Kingsley Ward. He wrote *"Letters of a Business Man to his Son"* and several years later, *"Letters of a Business Man to his Daughter,"* both excellent reads in how to succeed in Business and in life. In Letters to his Son, he devotes a whole chapter relating to how he defines Entrepreneur. I have extracted the following:

"To me, entrepreneurs are people with great imaginations. They seem too have answers for almost everything. No problems cannot be solved, no undertakings cannot be carried out. They are creative in their thinking, always seeking new methods of doing things. Their innate aptitude for avoiding the ordinary, the standard pathways of the business world is the very crux of their success." – G .Kingsley Ward.

I have previously defined my views about differentiating between a businessperson and an entrepreneur. One has to concede that generally they are two different types of people with the majority of the same business skills applying to both parties. An entrepreneur is a serial developer of ideas and/or companies, as opposed to the long-term developer of a specific business.

The entrepreneur will take more risks, with an insatiable appetite for continually assessing and challenging the 'status quo.' Entrepreneurs generally suffer from impatience, are not always the best at long term hands on management but more at home as the inspiration and driving force, the perfect 'change master.'

There is a very fine line that separates a successful entrepreneur from a successful businessperson. They are somewhat similar but the entrepreneurial personality generally has more energy, a more gambling spirit, are daring and certainly have less adherence to conventional business directions.

An entrepreneur faced with a limited amount of factual material or evidence to direct him/her will generally resort to gut feeling. Entrepreneurs are generally good at exploiting other people's ideas, the world is full of people with good ideas but they lack the conviction or the know-how to convert their ideas into a viable product or business.

It was John Doer, venture capitalist and early investor in Google, Amazon and Twitter who referred to Andre de Haes, Stanford Graduate School of Business with: "Entrepreneurs are a peculiar breed of human species."

It is my experience that most entrepreneurs have a natural ability to sell regardless of the value of the product that they are selling. It is the satisfaction of taking the order, even better when it is against competition, the desire to win is a very important part of the salesman's personality.

Maybe when selecting a candidate for a sales position you should challenge them to a game of Tennis or Squash and see how aggressive or determined they are (especially if they are losing) to win. Of course you may find on the other hand that they do not wish to beat their prospective boss for fear of not being selected!

Sales Representative, Commercial Traveller, Sales Executive, Sales Engineer, Sales Consultant, what is in a name? If it walks like a duck, talks like a duck, it's a duck! Whatever you call them or what they would like to be referred to, they are a Salesman (To be politically correct, Salesperson). Salesperson, if successful, should be one of the highest paid individuals in the company. You may baulk at this, but like any board director, they should be paid, on the basis of, part basic salary and part performance related bonus. If they are not successful then neither is your company!

A well-trained salesperson, both in sales techniques and product knowledge, motivated and ambitious with the right product and support, will succeed regardless of gender. I forgot who quoted me their definition of selling when they said, **"The transfer of the conviction from the mind of the seller to that of the buyer."** No, it was not my Granny but I have always felt that it was certainly the most basic of explanations. In other words, if the salesperson or person selling is not convinced of the merits/benefits of their product or service that he or she is selling, then, they will have an uphill struggle to convince the buyer. There is no difference between the Founder, Director, Telephone Receptionist or any other party if all of them can, when it comes to contacting the public/customer/client, make them believe in what they are selling or portraying about the product/company they work for. If you do not have that conviction/belief in the company/product, then it will be very difficult to get your message across.

Sales training is very important so is knowledge of the competition, their advantages and disadvantages. Remember it would be disastrous to start any marketing programme without first being organised and able to service the enquiries.

All my business life, I have corrected virtually every person who quotes 'Sales and Marketing' the emphasis being sales first then marketing. I was taught at a very early age by my mother that; **"Marketing creates and Sales satisfies"** in other words everything to do with marketing primarily, Research, PR,

Advertising – creates a demand for the product and, if successful, Sales convert that demand to orders.

So what's in a name?

Over the past 60 years, I have met many well-known, and justifiably labelled, Entrepreneurs. On the other hand, I have met substantially more of the one laying claim to the title, without the track record to back it up. The 90's saw the word Entrepreneur become a fashionable title or label to replace Businessperson, Woman, even Person. In my mind, it runs parallel to the use of the word Luxury when Real Estate agents in the 80's started to refer to specific apartments as Luxury. Now every apartment is defined as Luxury, regardless of the specificities!

Entrepreneur has become an all-purpose description for almost anyone who is in business, successful or otherwise; developer, shop owner, chef, financier, investor to name but a few, the list is endless. Do they all deserve to be recognized as Entrepreneurs? In my opinion, 'NO.' One success does not make you an Entrepreneur or as **MOGUS would say: "One Swallow does not make a summer."**

Are you starting a new business at 50 plus?

It's never too late. Let me tell you why I have got involved in a new start-up company and how it differs from starting the first company in my teens, early twenties and then my thirties.

Current stats show that there is an increasing number of new business start-ups initiated by the 50 plus population. Recent government statistics show that nearly 76% of retirees work post-retirement because they need the money and feel they still have something to offer – i.e., experience. Age or Gender is no barrier when starting a business or when realizing a dream. You just need fitness, patience and MONEY! The Office for National Statistics (ONS) states that the over 70's people make up 7 percent of business leaders and senior officials in the UK and there are approx. 528,000 people aged over 70 in employment in the UK, representing 1.6 per cent of all employed people aged 16 or over! I would quote 'The Times newspaper' in reference to Britain's success story that over the past decade the country has gone through an ENTREPRENEURIAL revolution with more than half a million businesses starting each year, reflecting nearly 2 per cent of the working population deciding to strike out on their own. It is quoted that some £12bn equity has been invested in private UK companies in 2019, a 58% percent increase on 2018 statistics (Source: Beauhurst).

The highs and the extreme lows – and the success & the failures and the price to be paid by friends and family alike. Whether you are 11 or 60+, fitness and health play a major part in developing a successful business. Above all, it is impossible to describe the enjoyment, and satisfaction experienced both from developing a successful company, and or product, from scratch but also seeing loyal staff who have worked tirelessly with you, during the good and bad times, meanwhile, also benefiting from the success of that company. No amount of money can, or ever will, surpass that feeling.

However, there are the lows of being associated with partners when fraud, deception and theft become apparent for their personal gain over partners and shareholders alike. Business fraud is, in many countries, endemic; researchers at the University of Chicago estimated that one in seven US companies is engaging in some kind of fraud costing investors about a fifth of the value of those companies.

Fraud now accounts for a third off all crime after four million offences were recorded last year (2020) in England and Wales. Fraud has risen in every region of the country with more than 12,000 incidents taking place every day. In the twelve months up to September, there had been a 61% increase in remote banking fraud and 27% in online shopping and auction's fraud (Quoted from Telephone-operated Crime Survey). GBG research reveals that more than 28% of businesses admit to high levels of fraud being accepted by the organization with over half (51%) of those seeing fraud attempt's rise in financial services.

Start as you mean to go on

In the early days of starting your company, you will be bombarded with advice, some good but the majority of them would be not so good. Not bad in the sense that it is wrong or inaccurate but more in the context of misleading. I will give you an example: You have to have the courage of your conviction, it is so easy to become distracted from the key issues and priorities; priorities at given times, as they are continually changing and must be updated or changed, according to circumstances. Creating, implementing and accepting the change are, in my mind, possibly the most difficult acts to internalize but the most rewarding and implicit to any business, be it new or established, small, large or global giant. Learn to love change as it can be very rewarding.

(MOGUS): **Failure is not falling down but refusing to get up. Start as you mean to go on!**

Some 55 odd years ago, I was rapped over the knuckles by my boss at the time, for making notes on any piece of paper that came to hand. Phone numbers, names, key points from telephone discussions, things I had to do, people to call and so on. Months, weeks, days even hours later, I could not find those scraps of paper with the information that I required. The temptation when on the phone or at an impromptu meeting to reach for the inevitable scrap of paper. DON'T DO IT – Use a day book (or phone/computer) and discipline yourself to use it for everything, including doodling. If you don't doodle in your day book, you will find a corner of paper to doodle on then the inevitable will happen, you will write a number or important message on the same paper. Your day book will be one of the most important aids that you will ever use and in my humble opinion, believe me, in this situation your computer will never replace the day book. The only addition when remembering to use the book for everything, is that every time you use a new page (even doodling), date it.

The first thing I do in the morning and the last thing at night is to check the day book for notes relating to actions that are required. I also have my computer phones and portable hard drives which of course I could not survive without. However, I have some 40 years of day books and 50 years of Business Diaries. I still refer to them. "Post-it" notes have a use but if their usage is not controlled, they will prove to be a disaster. I have lost count, over the years to the hundreds of colleagues that I have convinced to change their ways and without doubt for those who persevered, the day book has made their business life easier. **Start as you mean to go on.**

Finding the premises is both time-consuming and potentially costly. If your business can be started from home (even when there is no virus), that is good but do not fall into the bad habits of starting late because there was an interesting news item on the TV, do not need to shave to-day because I am working from home, wife or partner states, as you are at home you can do an early shop, friends call in as they see your car outside and so it goes on.

Working from home requires a discipline that most people whom I have ever met, including me, find it virtually impossible to continually maintain. It gets progressively worse if your partner is at home, after all, in an office environment the fleeting thoughts associated with the attractive colleague sitting opposite are generally brief. However, at home those thoughts can rapidly progress to reality and however enjoyable that may be, it is both disruptive and for the majority of us, (me included) time-consuming! **Start as you mean to go on.**

Serviced office accommodation can provide an alternative or bridge between homes and acquiring a dedicated commercial facility provided it is only temporary because it is not cheap when viewed in the long term. If you use this method, make sure that it fits your requirement and time constraints. Do not take on a long-term commitment or change your mind. **Start as you mean to go on.**

When taking on your first employees, "start as you mean to go on" takes on a whole new meaning. Employees need to be able to say, with a fair degree of certainty that the boss is; 'firm but fair,' we know where we stand, one rule for all, not them and us, keeps us in the picture (good and bad). I will quote an example here. In a growing business, staff can work many extra or unsociable hours, without pay. However, it is important to give and take and given that it is planned, those staff should be able to take time off in lieu.

What you do not want to happen is staff coming in late or going out on extended lunch breaks without them being planned. When I first approached a member of staff about these untimely events, I was met with a barrage of abuse that they were so committed to this company working all hours and you (meaning I) were being very ungrateful. My comment was that I do not have a problem with their taking time in lieu of hours. On the contrary, I would encourage it given that they understand that these leaves of absences, when taken without planning, can and will leave a shortfall in coverage as well as pressure on other members of staff that could so easily be avoided by communication. What should have happened, right at the beginning when the first person was employed that, time in lieu is not a problem providing it is communicated prior to, as opposed to post, the event. **Start as you mean to go on.**

There is nothing as demoralizing as working for a boss who continually changes his mind, priorities and values. There is probably one action or lack of it that is more demoralizing: a boss who cannot make up their mind or make a decision. Being indecisive is not the trait of an entrepreneur and neither should it be that of a businessperson. In fact, they would be better off as an employee rather than employer. I should also state that if you believe that your strategy or programme is wrong then stop and reassess it. Do not plough on because you do not wish to be proved wrong or accused of changing your mind. **Start as you mean to go on.**

Cash Flow. What is cash flow? The easiest description that I can give you is the difference between what you pay out (creditors) and what you receive (debtors) and when each of those actions occur. In extreme cases, like a bookmaker, where the provider of a service receives cash for his services prior to paying any possible benefactor (winner). If the horse loses, we would call this a positive cash flow to the bookmaker. Before you rush out to take bets, if the bookmaker gets his odds wrong (as an analogy or comparison the odds would be gross profit), he could pay out more than he has taken in, that would be a negative cash flow and if it persisted, this could mean disaster.

You can now probably start to appreciate that successful sales are only part of the equation. If the buyer takes a long time to pay, it can put a company into a difficult financial position, especially if their margins (gross profit) are small. On the other hand, if your debtors pay you promptly, you will have good gross profit margins and creditors are generous with their terms then your cash flow requirements could be minimal which in turn reflects on the amount of cash that you need to operate your business.

When setting out your business plan, you are introduced to cash flow and cumulative cash flow projections. These projections, forecast, crystal-ball gazing are key to a number of major decisions such as, how much money do I really need to borrow or require investment and when do I need it?

Prior to starting on these projections, you need to understand; the amount of gross profit that your product produces, the cost of the services and components that your company will need to purchase or contract i.e. communication services, rent rates, power etc. and the credit available (amount of time you can take before paying each account). In some cases, credit taken will have to be valued against cost paid as many companies will give a discount against early or prompt settlement of account.

Capital Equipment

This is a major factor in deciding how much money you need. Do you pay cash, lease purchase, lease, buy or credit purchase? If immediate cash is scarce then consider no-deposit leasing, but there is always a requirement for a number of months to be paid up front. I would seriously recommend that one does not go for lease hire as opposed to purchase. With hire, you are locked in for the two or three year period and at the end of that period, you have nothing to show for what you have paid. If at any time you decide that you need to reduce cash flow spend and have no immediate need of the equipment, you are locked in and cannot sell the equipment and will have to pay the difference, if there is a difference. Those contracts do not have a settlement figure that takes into consideration what you have already paid. You pay the contracted number of months outstanding plus a termination figure. For a start-up, they are not very flexible. Lease purchase probably gives you a more flexible approach when purchasing equipment. There are benefits relating to VAT and so called 'off balance sheet financing' but this would not affect a start-up position. Paying monthly or quarterly can make a difference to your cash flow requirements and should be viewed accordingly and don't forget changes in technology which can be rapid. 'What was acceptable yesterday can be obsolete and outdated by new technology today!'

I have quoted, and in some cases focused, on several accomplished Entrepreneurs, however, one outstanding British Entrepreneur who at 74 is still going strong in developing ideas into products and successful businesses is James Dyson. His dedication in developing a bag-less floor cleaner involved some 5,000 plus attempts, concluding successfully with prototype number 5,127 back in 1982.

Many other successful and diverse products have, and still are, being produced globally that have made Dyson a billionaire. Dyson has just had published his new book – *Invention: 'A Life by James Dyson'*. **(Ref: extracts from article "Portrait" by Stuart McClymont) Sunday Times Magazine.**

Feasibility Study/Research

A feasibility study or research, also referred to as the "Seed" is a brief description of what the product or service is, and what it provides, i.e. the benefits to whoever uses the product or service. Without a benefit being gained, your product will not sell. Every product or service, if acquired or used, must provide the buyer with a benefit. This does not mean if it is beautiful, wonderful, fantastic, and excellent or, "no home or even business should be without one." The Why, Where or What, make up the benefits. Unless you are selling flowers as they look great and smell lovely and make you happy to see them!

Competition, if appropriate, name the major or dominant force, briefly referring to any others. In a few words describe why your concept/product is better than your competitors, be it cheaper more efficient, etc.

Basic financials, such as cost of manufacture or provision (best estimate), selling price and market potential. This information should be sufficient to enable an investor to take an initial view as to the possibility and viability of your concept. The more factual the information or data presented, relative to the market place, the better understanding that both the investor and yourself will have as to the potential.

Present your data in no more than half a dozen pages, plus any support material like; independent analysis of markets, demographics, if relevant, editorials relating to market opportunities or problems that your concept may address, resolve or improve.

I believe that if you are at a stage where you are not sure of the potential for your product or idea and that prior to investing a great deal of time and/or resource you would like to approach an investor, affluent friend or possible manufacturer with a view to investment, be careful as to how much information you initially divulge before receiving a confirmed interest proceeded by a signed confidentiality agreement.

Generally, people fall into the trap of being product-led rather than market-led. So what's the difference? Product led endorses the comment 'I know it will sell' and unless you are blessed with being able to predict the future, you will find it almost impossible to raise funding for your project. Market-led is reflecting the benefits the product addresses in the market place locally, nationally and/or, globally.

However, it is not that unusual for a company to get carried away with a great idea by committing substantial recourses before realising that there is little or no demand for such a product. Let me put it in perspective before I am inundated by people quoting examples of product-led success like the Black and Decker Workmate, a universal work bench, the inspiration of its inventor who, allegedly trundled it around to many companies before a company could see its true potential. B&D was that company, the rest is history.

As for the Beatles, Brian Epstein vehemently believed in his product and that the time was right for their brand of music. Record company after record company turned them down as, 'too extreme and not right for the market.' As a music product, they were and still are, arguably one of the most successful of all time, thanks to Sir George Martin at EMI who signed them up. There are always exceptions. Although I am reliably informed that it is virtually impossible to find any person in the music industry who will admit to turning them down. Brian Epstein was without doubt an Entrepreneur, who although started out in the family business of selling records recognized an opportunity, had the passion and belief or as MOGUS would say, *"Have the courage of conviction to invest and stay with the product during the darkest days."*

For every product-led success, I can quote you a hundred market-led ones. If your initial research shows positive vibes, press on. If it has global possibilities, even better. Market-led products are still no guarantee of future market success, but they substantially reduce the risk of failing, or on the other hand, increase the chances of success! Investors, whatever shape or size they may come in, like to minimize their risk factor when investing and want to be convinced of the product's market potential. Use the courage of YOUR conviction, do not act on hearsay. However, if you find it interesting, then try to establish the foundation for such rumours or statements, it may just turn out to be useful.

Besides the Internet, which I believe is the greatest tool ever conceived for market research, especially when trying to establish if competition exists in the world. There is also an increasing number of companies who provide rapid research within twenty four/forty eight hours, for a relatively small amount of cash. Tweeting and social networking are also great marketing and research vehicles.

The Advertising Association in collaboration with NTC Publications provide an extensive number of invaluable marketing publications. Carrying out initial research is not a short haul especially if you are carrying out the feasibility whilst undertaking your normal day job, then recreation has to take a back seat. Although your initial idea may not be rocket science, it is worth remembering to, (MOGUS) *"keep your own council,"* divulge information on a 'need-to-no-basis' only. Obviously, if you are evaluating market potential, you have to divulge a certain amount of information. In certain cases, a simple non-disclosure agreement can prove invaluable.

If you have invented a product that shows positive potential, you would need to take advice from a patent agent. Provisional patent cover does not cost an arm or leg and should be considered whilst establishing whether the product has a future or not. Product trademark and/or brand registration together with Intellectual Property Registration becomes mandatory as it will protect and show confidence when consideration for licensing the idea, coupled with an initial feasibility report is ideal to present to the various parties for consideration. If you intend to go down this route, a simple confidentiality agreement is a necessity which provides a degree of protection.

Remember that everybody signs the confidentiality agreement before reading it or having a copy of it. That includes your longest and closest friend, even your father-in-law if he suggests that he may invest in it. Many a friendship and even divorce have been experienced because of the famous or should I quote those infamous words, "trust me I am a doctor" or (MOGUS) *'Start as you mean to go on,'* **though there are a very few exception**s.

Can a Confidentiality agreement be enforced? It depends on how much money you have, but probably in your situation, no. I would, however, still insist on having it completed, as it costs nothing, and one would have to question the motives of any party who refuses to acknowledge it. Besides, I believe it can act as a comforter to any future investor. Now the inevitable, and in my mind, one of the most critical aspects that can influence the project's success, regardless of the products viability, 'The Management Team.'

Whether you are looking for investment to fund a business, product development or feasibility study, you are primarily asking people to back you, your ability and judgment. Even if the investors are ecstatic about your proposal, they will turn the investment down if they are not convinced of your ability to manage the company or who the alternative would be to step in the event of illness or accident.

Your resume and that of any other party involved in the proposed development must form part of the feasibility. At this stage, it can be basic, stick to the past and present work experience, qualifications (if relevant) and achievements. This is not a job application and does not require listing your O & A level achievements, hobbies number of children and that you like carry curry and support Arsenal. Unless of course you have prior knowledge that the investor you are pitching to is a director of Spurs, then it may pay to be sycophantic and change your allegiance. The golden rule:

(MOGUS): *"Failure is not falling down but refusing to get up."*

Ask yourself, before presenting the initial feasibility study: what are you trying to achieve and what do you want from the investor? I have met with a number of parties over the years and found that 'loads of dosh' is their dominant inference when discussing their proposals. There is nothing wrong with that, in fact it is normally the major consideration of all parties, invariably though, their concept has not been properly thought through when relating to future plans for the company.

An investor needs to understand the options, relative to exiting their investment. Contrary to general belief, investors do not want to emulate "Father Xmas." They are investing money in exchange for equity in your company, (loans are also possible) and their investment in your project is only fulfilled when they can realize a profitable investment and in some cases if no dividends are forthcoming, an exit. This is normally considered at around three years or if exceedingly lucky, less.

If your thoughts are of building a long term business, without involving any further dilution by sale of your shareholding to an outside sources or possible IPO (public offering), then do not expect a rush of investors. (See section "do not fall in love with the company"). Entrepreneurs do not suffer with this problem. At the feasibility stage of your project, given that it has enabled you to achieve your objective of raising either, what I would refer to as seed capital and/or technical and marketing support, thereby allowing you to prove the viability of your project. You and/or your new partners are able to move to the next phase.

Setting out the stall for would be investors

During early 2019, the business plan was somewhat pushed to one side in favour of the "pitch deck," encompassing drag along rights etc. That's my own view because investors at that time were rarely using venture capital and generally producing simple funding documents for family, friends, bank or Angel investors. Things have changed somewhat as more money is required as is the scope for bigger and greater technology involvement coupled with the potential for more products to be in demand globally. The Business Plan is not only an introduction to the product and company, it is a living plan of your company now, and the future updated regularly by the executive board and or founders.

The Business Plan

Don't make it into a 'War and Peace' epic. You get judged on quality not quantity and furthermore remember, you are not preparing a wish list!

- ➢ Incorporate an index with numbered pages. Each section divider identified by either an alphabetic icon or number.
- ➢ You need several hard copies. Do not use a slide-on-spine, have them ring bound, if possible.
- ➢ Front and back cover, use a coloured, matt or gloss card with title printed. This is not a big cost from a high street printing/copying company.
- ➢ If you have graphs or data sheets remember to identify the source and date of that information. Non-credited information is worthless!
- ➢ Disclosure agreement, an example of this page with suggested text is in 'Trouble Shooters Archive.'
- ➢ Confidentiality agreement (Available as above)
- ➢ Copies of artwork or visual examples relating to your product if they are not black and white re-produce as colour copies and include. Any promotional literature, photographs that exists together with press releases and any independent acknowledgements re market, concept and competition.

> ➤ Inside cover sheet, pre index, to quote copyright and restrictions on these without prior agreement (see trouble shooters archive) Remember to number each business plan and to record who they are given to and request their return if not of interest.

> ➤ Power point presentation, on line video are all important visual aids in getting your story across to an investor.

The Business plan should be easy to read with a clear and well produced copy. Do not crowd the page with small text and finally, what is very important 'PROOF READ' the finished product prior to any person receiving it regardless of it being available either online or as hard copy. A minimum of two people should read the copy, one of the two people should not be party to the business as more often than not, you understand what has been written because you are the major contributor, but I can predict that the non-involved person who reads it will come across statements, that to the non-initiated, make no sense at all. Proof reading is a skill borne of time; if you can, choose somebody who is used to producing or constructing agreements or copy, all the better. The end product is a reflection of the effort and preparation that has gone into the plan, remember the definition of luck?

(MOGUS') **Don't spoil the ship for a 'Harpeth of tar.'**

The saying means, do not compromise the quality of the finished product in order to save a few pence or cents. Your business plan reflects you, your product, and if operational, your company. The ease of reading your plan goes a long way towards the credibility of your proposal and the people or person behind it.

There is no dyed in the wool structure for a business plan other than the obvious requirements of product, management, market, competition and financials. I have seen plans with extremely complex financial analysis data that take the investors through to copious pages describing the product.

I have found that the common factor with the vast majority of plans that I have seen is a revenue forecast that should be halved, expenditure that should be doubled and the optimistic time period projected for the company to reach positive cash flow, let alone profit, is generally well adrift of the forecast.

So let us go through each section that I found meets everybody's requirements or perhaps I should say, nearly everybody. There is always one!

Introduction

Use a maximum of single page, describe what you are trying to achieve in reference to the financial investment, joint venture or partnership. If the project is a new company start up, or at an early stage investment opportunity (company operational for a limited period of time with initial investment to date, by existing director or directors) this can also be part of the: **Executive Summary, which is as important as the BP itself.**

Executive Summary – **(**see page 92**)** has to reflect all the key points in the Business plan. Remember this copy, when used separately as a pathfinder to the business plan, has to sell You, Your company and Your Idea, generally without you being present. It is what it says, a summary. No need to include detailed information covering research, and sales. Just write a summary using one page or two at max, describe in about 500 words the following;

1. Company objectives
2. Product
3. Market
4. Future
5. Why you believe the company will succeed (Remember positives not adjectives)
6. Brief resume of you and/or partners

The Product

What is the product or service, its benefits, users and if relevant, subscribers. How you intend to manufacture or produce the product. Length of time involved in development. If company is not formed or trading, feedback from initial research test marketing, evaluation or, some or all of the relevant parts of the **feasibility study,** if produced.

The Market

Economic and demographic data; Consumer targeting classification (Information, if available, from the: Advertising Competition, Marketing and Sales Association, NTC Publications).

Sales forecast & Implementation

1. Financials
2. Sales Revenue
3. Operational costs
4. Cumulative Cash Flow
5. Projected P&L

(See cash flow is king.)

Appendices:

Selected copies of articles, photographs, supporting correspondence that promotes or endorses the product or its market potential. Number each item, as you may wish to refer to this supporting information in other areas of the business, e.g. marketing.

Business plan is primarily produced for two reasons: To establish the business objectives of the company and to raise capital & investment. In turn, the Business Plan should both reflect and focus on you and your fellow directors in developing ideas, products and the company. At the same time, projecting future financial requirements and growth opportunities both organically and/or by acquisition. The Business Plan should project the next or first three years of the company' plans and be part of **an annual, ongoing review and update by the board of directors.**

The Business Plan should also be the blueprint for the future, accurately (generally very difficult for a start-up) reflecting all aspects of the company's business, warts and all. It is a constant reminder of the objectives being targeted and the budgets agreed and should be constantly reviewed and updated as a board document. Some investor's request a five-year forecast. I will never be convinced that five years is viable in developing any form of projection. I have yet to see a five-year forecast that to date has ever been achieved; therefore I believe it is unrealistic for any investor to request such figures. Three years is viable and essential. Again, in a start-up, it is possible to take an overview of what the three years projections and developments hold.

Business Plans **come in all shapes and sizes good, bad, indifferent and very bad.** I believe that, depending on the stage that a person is at, (relative to the viability of the product and to what extent the market has been researched), that it can be useful to consider three separate stages, up to and completing the Business Plan. If the product or concept is, I hate using the word, 'unique' and seemingly without any form of competition, then I would suggest a basic feasibility study/report is produced. This can also be the forerunner for the next part of the business plan:

an edited key summary of the BP called the **"Executive Summary."**

The Executive Summary & the Three "C's"

Compact, Constructive and Credible. An executive summary is arguably the most important document as it is generally read prior to any potential investor wishing to meet and/or discuss, in greater detail, the company or proposal. From my experience, the Executive Summary, is the most read section (financials aside) of the Business Plan. It has to sell your product, business projected cash flow and investor benefits, in no more than two pages of A4 paper. Besides being the introduction to your business plan, it is the investor's first exposure to you and your proposal.

I am a great believer in its use as a **Pathfinder document,** a stand-alone promotional aide, used to establish investor interest, prior to agreeing the release of the full business plan. Yes I do mean, agreeing to release. Your business plan is an insight to your company, encompassing confidential information and data. Never to be circulated indiscriminately or, if you excuse the phrase, "for whoring around investors." The investment market place (we will examine these parties later) are comparatively close-knit and if they hear a proposal is "doing the rounds," then they will generally avoid being party to the proposal, as though it were the plague. It has been my experience that investors, as a generalisation, like to believe that they are the first to be approached.

How do we go about achieving our goals and what marketing tools do we need to do it? The marketing mix to be considered, when planning and budgeting: Product Name/Brand, Stationary, Website Audible Image, Point of sale material i.e., Literature, Display Giveaways etc., Advertising, Direct Mailing, Promotion, Exhibitions, Public Relations, Endorsement, Sponsorship, Staff.

Product Name or Brand?

The Brand and what it stands for is misunderstood by many; like the name in a stick of rock, the brand influence runs right through your company. The brand is a promise to the recipient of the product. This promise must be understood and endorsed by every member of your staff. There can be no exceptions. Your office and or factory, company ethics, and policies must also endorse and reflect what the brand stands for. The brand is a guarantee of confidence, commitment, and trust. The logo, creative style, marketing, and sales approach visually reflect the brand. Regular audits by the company are imperative to ensure that everyone endorses the brand, especially if you want your brand to be a promise, not a disappointment.

I have, to a degree, tried to cover the importance of the product name in the earlier text. How does this differ from the brand? For example, Black & Decker is a brand name the B&D Workmate is or was a product name. What comes first? It depends on the product. In developing Shanning, the healthcare group I was involved with, the first company was Shanning International Ltd, a hospital equipping company. As Shanning's name developed internationally, Shanning became synonymous with Healthcare in its specific field. New products and companies developed from Shanning; POD, Healthcare, Mobility, Lasers, etc. The brand was Shanning; the products had their own sales identity and model prefix, relative to that company's development.

I would like to think that the "Shanning brand" did become synonymous with quality and reliability in the healthcare industry .....Globally.

It is not necessary to start a new company with every product, and if the product sits comfortably within the core business, then it becomes a division which is where it should be. However, some products result from collaboration between companies until such time that it makes sense to move it from a division to a standalone company/ subsidiary or at the right price. A sale!

Referred to as brand extension or "brand stretch," a good example is Virgin, whose brand features in many named products. The early brand was specifically music & entertainment; now, it may be referred to as a conglomerate. You have to be careful of weakening or devaluing the brand by wide and varied use outside its core business.

This can be detrimental to its value, thereby affecting its strength, long-term viability, credibility, and if it is a public company, share price! Any adverse publicity can have a knock-on effect on other companies bearing that brand name. Of course, there is a PR value when related to positive publicity, reflecting on all the companies bearing that brand name. The "easy Group" is an interesting and, without a doubt, unique (correctly used in this instance) company. You associate the "easy brand" with; low cost, economic, value

S-curves are **good graphical project management tools for planning, monitoring, controlling, analysing,** and **forecasting a**

project's status & performance. They show work progress over time and form a historical record of project trends and variations. Followed by tapering or levelling off. The tapering occurs when the population of new and existing customers declines. At this point, growth is slow and or non-existent, ringing alarm bells that a review of the product or its development is long overdue. It has always figured in my mind as part of a company's tool for "CHANGE." Why are so many people/companies reluctant to implement and or accept CHANGE in their companies' development and, in many cases, their own way of life? CHANGE is a book on its own, and I have to say that in 1985 I was given a book by Doctor Rosa Beth Moss Kantar called – "Change Masters," which I found enlightening and a wonderful guide when reviewing the positives and the negatives of a developing and developed company regardless of its size. I include a number of points extracted from "Change Master Publications' that I believe are mandatory.

(MOGUS): **To improve is to change; to be perfect is to enhance. (Winston Churchill)**

"Clear Change" - Goals

Like a medical practitioner, you would begin by diagnosing the real issues and then proposing clear "goal-directed" solutions. He/she will begin by analysing:

> The existing problems or issues.
> The current reality and efficiency of the organisation/division.
> The desired future ideal position.
> The barriers preventing the organisation from achieving that desired position.
> The forces for change that exist within the organisation.
> The dreams, goals, and values of the key stakeholders within the organisation
> The organisation's future strategy, financial projections and costs
> The organisation's values.
> The organisation's readiness and capacity for change.
> Changes occurring in the organisation's external environment that may impact on the organisation and its customers.

This information will determine the type of change required by the Organisation/Company.

(MOGUS): The first step towards change is awareness. The second step is acceptance. – Nathaniel Brandun

Enterprising Oldies

Founding new businesses is not a monopoly of the young, even if it seems so nowadays. "A LAZY bastard living in a suit" was Leonard Cohen's description of himself in a new album, but there was no sign of his laying down his guitar. He spent 2008-10 on tour, performing on stage in Barcelona on his 75th birthday. "Old Ideas" have won widespread acclaim.

In the 1960s, pop was a young person's business. 'The Who' hoped they died before they got old. Bob Dylan berated middle-aged squares like Mr Jones in "Ballad of a Thin Man." But today, age is no barrier to success. The Rolling Stones are still touring in their 70s. Bob Dylan's song writing skills, if not his vocal cords, have survived intact. Sir Paul McCartney warbles on music explode and Tom Jones at 80 has never been better.

It is time to enterprise what such ageing rockers have done for pop music. This idea has been powerfully reinforced by the latest tech boom: Facebook, Google and Groupon where all founding people were in their 20s or teens. Mark Zuckerberg, aged 27, will soon be able to count his years of worth in billions, not millions, of dollars. But the trend is not confined to tech: Michael Reger was a founder of one of America's most innovative energy companies, Northern Oil and Gas, aged 30.

This is not to say that the rise of young entrepreneurs like Mark Zuckerberg is insignificant. The barriers that once discouraged enterprise among the young are collapsing, if not collapsed! Social networks make it easier to build contacts. Knowledge-intensive industries require relatively little capital. But the fact that barriers are collapsing for the young does not mean that they are being erected for greybeards. The point is that the creation of fast-growing businesses is now open to everybody regardless of age or gender.

Back on the road again

The evidence that older people are becoming more enterprising should help to calm two of the biggest worries that hang over the West (and indeed over an ageing China and Japan). One is that the greying of the population will inevitably produce economic sluggishness. The second is that older people will face hard times as companies shed older workers in the name of efficiency and welfare states cut back on their pensions.

Let us hope the same is true of the ageing boomers who will have little choice but to embrace self-employment as the West's welfare states discover that they cannot keep their promises let alone addressing the global changes relating to the Covid-19 Virus.

Over 50s make up almost half of all self-employed workers in 2019, the total of 2.2 million is according to the jobs and advise web site 'Rest Less' likely to increase significantly in 2020 with Covid prevailing. The analysis showed that in 2019 there were fewer than five million self-employed workers of whom 2.26 million were aged over 50. The Office for National Statistics states that the self-employed are on average older than employees, and among workers over the age of 34, more financially resilient than employees.

I would quote a statement made in The Times article titled, *"That Confidence Trick" by Anna Jordan relating to Female Entrepreneurs:*

"When you strike out as an entrepreneur, there's nobody for you to check in with or who will say yes, what are you doing is right or no, what you are doing is wrong," comments Jordan. "There's no boss - it's just you. You don't have that validation or support from a network. "And how can you feel confident and secure if you are the only person you know who's ever tried to do it?"

It is my opinion that it is a very viable quote and relevant to both Men and Women alike.

However (MOGUS): *"Success is never permanent; failure is never fatal."* **(Sir Winston Churchill)**

Key points to remember when starting a business

1. 'Register company name followed by domain name as a priority.

Intellectual Property (IP) is very important for any company, let alone a new one and often overlooked which can have significant effect on the company's valuation. A company needs to protect both its IP, the possibility of patents and trademarks which are all parts of supporting a company's goals (that must be reflected in the company's Business plan). Even AI (Artificial Intelligence) can be Patented.

Patents are more than just protecting a company's assets; they are valued as a major tool for business growth and market dominance.

2. Remember, you sell benefits, no benefit means no viable product – no product means, no company!

3. "Product-led not Market-led."

4. Regardless of the company's size, you have to **implement Corporate Governance.** Corporate governance is the system of rules, practices, and processes by which a company is directed and controlled. Corporate governance essentially involves balancing the interests of a company's shareholders, senior management executives, customers,

suppliers, financiers, the government, and the community. Corporate governance is about what the board of a company does, its values forms part of the day-to-day management of the company. Effective governance also provides benefits as it improves both transparency and accountability beyond the corporate sector.

5. Appoint accountants, as soon as possible, – commencing with bookkeeping.

6. Keep records of expenditure and when possible, revenue, from day 1.

7. Never ignore the importance of cash flow.

8. Exercise every day, even a walk home, as stress is a killer!

9. Involve staff and shareholders in regular updating sessions and the PR value of positive news.

10. Remember the **Peter's principal: "Promoting a person to a level of incompetence."** In many cases, there is always a key member of staff who performs their role to a high degree of competence within the company and is considered for promotion! Now THINK, if they were great in their previous role but they fail in the promotion, what do you do? Dismiss them because their previous role has been replaced by a competent person? It happens and in many ways you can make the move as a temporary one,

pending a review and then that person will not lose face if the role is not for them.

Finally, **Remember** the **Change: S -Curve & Business Plan Reviews.**

(MOGUS): **Remember when life seems difficult, there is a light at the end of every tunnel, just hope it's not coming from a train!**

Business fraud or fraud for life?

Definition of Fraud (*Oxford Languages*):

Wrongful or criminal deception intended to result in financial or personal gain – a person or thing intended to deceive others typically by unjustifiably claiming or being credited with accomplishments or qualities.

You may ask what fraud has got to do with you.

Fraud has become endemic throughout the world we live in, the problem is how one defines fraud. In my business career, I have encountered many aspects of fraud that have caused serious and in certain cases, disastrous results to that business and/or to me personally. Of course, the party creating the fraud may call it by another name for instance: Commission, which can be interpreted in two different ways: a) commission on sales or b) payment for influencing or arranging a sale (sometimes referred to as bribery).

Corporate purchasing is prone to such problems specifically advertising the World Federation of Advertisers predicts Ad fraud by 2025 costing the industry $50 billion a year. There are many opportunities for the development and introduction to Ad-verification tools and as more channels become digitally connected the opportunity for fraud gets even greater. These areas pose a major problem for Chief Marketing Officers especially as they have to encourage and introduce new innovation to their company and clients. They must ensure that they and their board including shareholders understand the many forms that Ad-Fraud takes and the availability of technology to address this growing and expensive problem.

I quote Cybercrime as one of the most serious frauds to grow especially in a pandemic. Scams and fraud relating to:

a) URL's: 1 in 10 are Malicious.

b) E-mails: 1 in 412 sent are identified as malicious.

c) 1 in 3,207 emails are phishing emails.

Ref: (Symantec / Broadcom)

a) *Voice fraud by phone; $14bn lost to phone fraud globally each year*

b) *Increase in contact centre fraud in last five years 350%.*

c) *41% of customers blame the brand for fraud happening.*

d) *20% of all posts about fashion products on Instagram feature counterfeit and / or illicit products*

(Ref Raconteur 2020 &
Ghost date)

Top brands mentioned by Counterfeiters: *Analysis of nearly 700,000 Instagram posts from counterfeiters containing hashtags or related* *hashtags of some of the top 16 fashion houses in the world range from Gucci at 16% to Versace at 3%.*

According to *'CyberEdge2020,* 'Global IT' decision makers took the following actions after they were victimised by ransomware in the 12 months to November 2019.

a) *Paid ransom to recover data: 66.9%*

b) *Paid ransom but lost data: 33.1%*

c) *Did not pay ransom and recovered data: 84.5%*

d) *Did not pay ransom and lost data: 15.5%*

If during the development, operation and expansion of your company and you as the founder/CEO have no shareholders, and or, investors and have not committed any aspect of fraud as defined in the definition, then in my view, I believe you would, however small, have committed a fraud – as defined above.

However, the seriousness of ones actions grow when they effect other people i.e., shareholders, Investors, Inland Revenue, Customers, corporate law/ governance, fraud squad. I have personally experienced serious fraud carried out knowingly by shareholders and Directors alike in companies that I have previously invested in as well as being a director and non-executive chairman.

I have also been party to implementing commission payments to in-country agents in respect to contracts carried in that country. In many countries, it is compulsory when carrying out business to be represented by an agent who is a resident in that country. They are involved in your discussions with the potential client when tendering and during the contract period. To be fair, the right agent can be instrumental in introducing new enquiries. Agency Commissions are paid against the award and completion of successful contracts. I have no doubt that in certain cases that commission is distributed to parties assisting the Agent!

Fraud under the bribery act can inflict substantial damage to the company, its brand image and global reputation.

investigated by the fraud office with some paying the penalties and/or others suffering reputation damage. I was personally party to such fraud when as a Name at Lloyds of London, established in 1686 and is now the world's biggest insurance market, the syndicate that I was party to collapsed due to millions of pounds being misappropriated when the main partners plundered the insurance syndicates for millions of pounds and then skipped the country to live in the USA where both died some years later. As a name, you are responsible for the amount that you have pledged to underwrite. That cost to all names in that Syndicate, me included, was millions of pounds. It was reported that some elderly names committed suicide as they had to sell everything they owned to pay their dues as a name on that syndicate.

GBG, the world's largest identity and fraud data eco system, claims that fraud has hit a high thanks to Covid 19 – one in five consumer identities have been stolen and one in three are more worried about fraud. GBG also states that 28% of businesses admit to high level of fraud being accepted by the organisation with 51% of those in financial services seeing fraud attempts rise. That is another reason why behavioural biometrics and pattern recognition come to the rescue.

Has fraud in business changed? No, and in many cases, it's not necessarily the size of the fraud as theft of company assets is, in my experience, "par for the course" with the attitude that **"I own the company and I can do what I wish with expenses and cash payments" to name but a few!** NOT IF YOU HAVE SHAREHOLDERS and/or INVESTORS. If one does, then you are unlikely to be able to obtain investment ever again as references are so important when looking for credit and/or investment.

Money, Money, Money

I quote the enterprise allowance scheme that was set up in 1983 by Margaret Thatcher's government, where funds were made available to those who were not then-employed and had a viable business idea. That went on to fund more than 325,000 individuals. The scheme was said to support Entrepreneurship during a period of major unemployment. It was believed that one in every six of the start-ups taking part failed in their first year and made no major dent in unemployment as most of the businesses created were sole trading operations, with over 75,000 being under 25.

The new scheme proposed would target the under 30's with a viable business proposal and access to £2,000 in start-up capital. I would encourage any participant to produce a good and feasible "Executive Summary" (See page 92), because it is the key to your presentation.

New Business Opportunities?

A lot of people ask if there are any areas/sectors which look "HOT" for future development opportunities. If I knew that, I would be worth a fortune, however, I do believe Healthcare to be that HOT sector which of course has many related business opportunities, specifically in audio/visual communications between patient and medical professional, the same communication is also in great demand between the vet and animal owner.

Are there areas/trends/sectors from Vet and Animal owner's especially Green trends, relating to climate change. In June 2021, in a communication to its investors, Credit Suisse stated that they were projecting this market (Green Market) to grow by some 30% over the next 9 years with a prediction that it could grow from $1.4 billion as of 2021 to $1.4 trillion by 2050. Astonishingly, from the $5.9 billion raised over the past decade more than half was in 2020, the year of global pandemic!

1. New ideas for digital advertising in a "Cookie-less" world: US digital advertising market is larger than the GDP of more than two thirds of the world's countries with 60% plus benefited by Google and Facebook! (ref Quantcast)
2. Global Gaming community estimated to rise above 3 billion in 2023, a forecast that has ample opportunities for brand integration.

3. Any areas where time/travel can be all but eliminated will be in big demand as a product service. Garden development in relation to leisure facilities and green facilities for decoration on balconies will, I believe, be a growth market.

4. Anything that saves time when introduced. Time is money!

5. Green related ideas, products or issues that are able to reflect green benefits to specific services and/or products reflect economic and social value. This targets both companies and governments alike.

6. Artificial Intelligence and wearables (AI) play an important role in the changing face of workplace learning which means interactive training (all part of soft-skills training i.e. learning and development) opportunities prevail. I quote (ref Gartner, 2019) – AI is predicted to drive $2.9 trillion in business value in 2021 i.e. 13% Smart products, 44% Decision support/augmentation, 19% Decision automation and 24% Agents.

AI's ability to identify and learn from data patterns and translate them into useful technologies has and is proving to be indispensable for many companies and sectors such as healthcare and providers of medical services i.e. robotic cleaners, sanitisers and delivery services, to name but a few. Market predictions (Grand View) predict that the market will be worth $390+ billion by 2025 indicating a growth of 46.2 % since 2019 (Rebecca Stewart Raconteur). Supporting this opportunity is another statistics which says, half of all work tasks will be handled by machines by 2025 (World Economic Forum forecast).

We must not forget opportunities, such as Biometric ones, as the majority of humans (age prevailing) begin to understand the limitations of passwords with the opportunities that digital identity can provide especially in Identification with regards to fraud, travel, etc. One in five consumers were affected by identity fraud in 2020 (Ref GBG).

According to research carried out in 2019, by Paysafe in North America and Europe, the advantage of using Biometrics over other authentication methods is that they are:

- 44% faster
- 44% More convenient
- 37% More secure
- 25% No need for phone or other service
- 23% Not good at remembering passwords
- 15% Can make purchases while doing other things
- 16% None of these reasons.

Improvisation

To me, there is no greater example of Entrepreneurial opportunism than the Entrepreneur who bought all Bernie Madoff 's **(US Hedge-fund investment manager sentenced in 2009 to 150 years for defrauding investors of $50 billion)** under pants from the official receiver and made them into I-Pad covers selling at $500 a cover. They were an instant hit especially to those in the financial sector!

It was in February 2020 that my associates and I were looking at the opportunities relating to the provision of Masks in relation to Covid-19 and the panic globally about the shortage of the relevant masks etc. As my Company VIIL had over twenty years of experience in dealing in China, healthcare being one area, we discussed provision of quality face masks with several established in-country manufactures that we dealt with relating to other healthcare products. Whilst discussing the opportunities, I also contacted several parties involved in material purchases for the Mayor's office with a view to establish an opportunity to quote for quantity supply of disposable masks that were manufactured to EU standards. On the three occasions that I actually got to speak to a party in the Mayor's office, I was advised that their requirements for transport, police, fire and ambulance were being handled by the government directly as part of the overall requirement for all services and the NHS but they would keep me informed and if appropriate, forward the information discussed.

We are now all aware of what happened and the benefits to specific parties!

However, Bernie Madoffs under pants made me think: could my M&S, Autograph pants convert to a face mask? The pants are made of a fine Polyester material with wide elasticated rib. After numerous attempts. I found a perfect way to put them on my face and they worked a treat... I wore them for a week and told my friends of their benefits and ease of wearing. I took a photo and sent it to a few friends. Any negative results? Yes, when shopping in a major supermarket, I received a phone call, and after a few seconds, I realised it was difficult to hear the person calling. I remember saying, "I can't hear you, I need to take my pants off" to which a woman walking past me smiled and said "I can't wait for this!" Another opportunity lost? **Every day produces an idea, just spend time thinking "how can I convert that into an opportunity?"**

In Conclusion

The number of self-employed workers has been increasingly steady since 2015. However, the growth has slowed sharply to 9.1% from a peak 11.2% at the start of 2020 (Source ONS).

Looking back on the entrepreneurial efforts of developing the numerous companies and projects over a 50-year period, I have come to the conclusion that the one repeated failing during the later years of expanding the companies was a lack of delegation at the top. I was lucky at an early stage of developing companies in the role of Chairman & CEO. One of my partners, Ron Bottling, played such a huge role as the group Chairman/ Financial Director. Ron was a highly experienced FCA and businessman when he invested in Shanning and then after several years, he came on full-time enabling me as CEO to concentrate on the development and expansion of the companies and projects as the CEO. Without doubt, there were a few decisions that were not made and they should have been. It affected the development and efficiency which in turn had negative effects on that company's development and in several cases led to premature cessation that in my view should be laid at the door of the then-Chairman/CEO, Ken Burgess.

This is without doubt a factor born of Entrepreneurs but must be rectified ASAP when developing more than one company and/or projects. It was interesting to read that Elon Musk made that transition recently when he relinquished his role of Chairman and CEO at Tesla to CEO.

I hope you will find the book interesting and informative in assisting you in taking up a role as an Entrepreneur or alternatively deciding that this is not for you.

When my sons were old enough (pre & post University) and interested in working with their Father, they experienced the rough with the smooth, the highs and the lows, the late nights and early mornings. They also went their own way in entrepreneurial pursuits, some good and some not so good. They persevered and I am very proud to say that they are both very successful in their own endeavours as Entrepreneurs, Creative Strategists, Writers and Humanitarians and not least – Parents.

I am not a religious person in that I do not worship any particular religious deity. However, that does not mean to say that I am an Atheist. If I have to describe my feelings I would say that I am an Agnostic and therefore I appreciate that most people would say that I am a "Cop- Out." I honestly cannot make up my mind and having travelled extensively around the world, meeting all types of people and in many cases, making true friends with people from all persuasions. I have to admit that if I was alone in a boat in the middle of an ocean and it was slowly sinking I would probably say "God, please help me I do not wish to die."

With all the turmoil in the world My Old Granny would say:

(MOGUS) "When you climb the ladder of success, may you never meet a friend."

For years I could not understand this statement. I thought it was selfish until one day **MOG** sat me down and said,

"When your achievements are growing, whatever they may be, don't forget your friends, especially if they are experiencing the opposite of your success; hopefully you will not experience this but if you do, be there for them!"

BE A FRIEND AND DON'T FORGET THEM

With the current and developing technology available, virtually any new business venture can address a global market. I have found that it is so important to be able to communicate in a manner that is acceptable to nearly all people regardless of Location, Language, Colour, Creed and Gender and not forgetting – Age.

I was given the print (on the following page) named 'DESIDERATA' some years ago as the person who owned it had died and his Daughter (Liz Cooper) was clearing out his garage, I was helping her and we discovered the print. I could not stop reading it as it reflected (300+ previous years) so many thoughts, views and frustrations that I felt where and feel sure that most people have, will or currently are, experiencing in their life time especially with the current problems being experienced in Croatia/Europe

(MOGUS): **"No matter what ever you achieve, there will always be critics.**

On the Bottom of the print is a very faint inscription of the *FOUND IN OLD SAINT PAUL'S CHURCH, BALTIMORE DATED 1692.'*

DESIDERATA

GO PLACIDLY AMID THE NOISE & HASTE, & REMEMBER WHAT PEACE THERE MAY BE IN SILENCE. AS FAR AS POSSIBLE WITHOUT surrender be on good terms with all persons. Speak your truth quietly & clearly; and listen to others, even the dull & ignorant; they too have their story. Avoid loud & aggressive persons, they are vexations to the spirit. If you compare yourself with others, you may become vain & bitter; for always there will be greater & lesser persons than yourself. Enjoy your achievements as well as your plans. Keep interested in your own career, however humble; it is a real possession in the changing fortunes of time. Exercise caution in your business affairs; for the world is full of trickery. But let this not blind you to what virtue there is; many persons strive for high ideals; and everywhere life is full of heroism. Be yourself. Especially, do not feign affection. Neither be cynical about love; for in the face of all aridity & disenchantment it is perennial as the grass. Take kindly the counsel of the years, gracefully surrendering the things of youth. Nurture strength of spirit to shield you in sudden misfortune. But do not distress yourself with imaginings. Many fears are born of fatigue & loneliness. Beyond a wholesome discipline, be gentle with yourself. You are a child of the universe, no less than the trees & the stars; you have a right to be here. And whether or not it is clear to you, no doubt the universe is unfolding as it should. Therefore be at peace with God, whatever you conceive Him to be, and whatever your labors & aspirations, in the noisy confusion of life keep peace with your soul. With all its sham, drudgery & broken dreams, it is still a beautiful world. Be careful. Strive to be happy.

Printed in Great Britain
by Amazon

85825040R00071